THE
Tarot
Bible

THE
Tarot
Bible

THE DEFINITIVE GUIDE TO
THE CARDS AND SPREADS

Sarah Bartlett

STERLING

New York / London
www.sterlingpublishing.com

8 9 10

Published in 2006 by Sterling Publishing Co., Inc.
387 Park Avenue South, New York, NY 10016
Distributed in Canada by Sterling Publishing
c/o Canadian Manda Group, 165 Dufferin Street,
Toronto, Ontario, Canada M6K 3H6

First published in Great Britain in 2005 by
Godsfield Press, a division of
Octopus Publishing Group Ltd
2–4 Heron Quays, London E14 4JP, England

Sterling ISBN-13: 978-1-4027-3838-8

For information about custom editions, special
sales, premium and corporate purchases, please
contact Sterling Special Sales Department at
800-805-5489 or specialsales@sterlingpub.com.

Contents

Introduction

The tarot has been used over the centuries to divine the future and to discover hidden truths. Not so long ago it was given a bad press, shunned by the Church, considered evil or doom-laden and became associated with the darker occultist arts. Yet over the past 30 years or so the tarot has grown in popularity again and has become one of the major tools for self-discovery and personal growth. Why? Perhaps the answer is simple—the tarot speaks a language that is accessible to all.

The 78 cards in the tarot deck carry an extraordinary ability to mirror who you are. They provide an immediate access to your deeper self too, whether you call this your intuition, soul, inner guide, divine messenger or guardian angel. The tarot "speaks" a language that is universal because it taps into the archetypal realms that permeate your unconscious. These are universal qualities that are the most basic patterns of human feelings, ideas and thoughts.

This definitive guide to the tarot is for beginners and more advanced practitioners alike. Divided into two parts, it offers easy access to both its interpretations and practicalities.

The world of tarot

Part 1 provides an easy entry into the world of tarot, covering the basics. It provides you with an understanding about its background and roots. You can find out what it is and what it isn't, where the tarot came from and why it works. You will also find out the benefits it can bring to your personal development, both as a pathway to finding a meaning in

Tarot is a unique tool for self-understanding and for making choices about the future.

life which is specific for you and for psychological growth, self-awareness and making choices for your future.

The structure of the tarot deck is fully explained in these initial pages and there are descriptions of the more popular decks that have been used throughout history. You might find this useful to refer to when selecting your own set of cards.

Using the tarot

Within the main body of the book is a directory, which is divided into eight chapters covering various topics. "Getting started" includes step-by-step instructions for using the tarot and includes information on how to choose a

There are many different designs of tarot deck to choose from.

pack, rituals and shuffling techniques. It outlines how to ask questions and, most importantly, provides exercises and guidelines for interpretation and developing your intuition. There is information on reversed cards and also a discussion about the power of psychological "projection" when reading the cards.

The following chapter includes complete interpretations, key words and phrases for every tarot card of the Major Arcana, while the next chapter offers comprehensive and focused interpretations of those cards in the tarot which are often overlooked or given very brief overviews in many books.

The next four chapters provide a wide variety of tarot layouts you can try for yourself: they cover everyday, relationship, revelation and destiny spreads. Starting off with the most basic—two-card and three-card spreads, favorite cards and self-discovery layouts—you can move on to more in-depth readings. There are relationship spreads you can do on your own or with a partner, and further revelation spreads for personal development. Finally, there are more complicated and traditional spreads such as the Celtic cross, astrology, gypsy, zodiac and year-ahead spreads.

The concluding chapter tells you how to develop your skills and increase your knowledge. It includes practical ways to combine the tarot with numerology, crystals and the Kaballah, with further techniques for developing greater insight into interpretations.

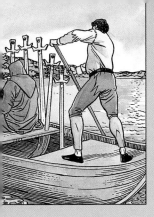

Part 1

Tarot basics

What is tarot?

The tarot is a deck of 78 mystical cards. There are 22 cards that form the Major Arcana and represent individuals who personify a particular quality or archetype. The 56 cards of the Minor Arcana represent events, people, behavior, ideas and activities that go on in our lives. For hundreds of years the tarot has been one of the most important Western mystical pathways for fortune-telling, divination and self-development. With connections to alchemy, psychology, astrology, numerology, Kaballah, Christian mysticism, Eastern philosophy and many other esoteric traditions, the tarot is available to everyone. It is a mirror of the human soul.

A universal language

Each card has an image, a name and a number, which are potent symbols and have specific meanings. At its simplest level, tarot is a universal language that speaks through a variety of archetypal symbols. Getting to know the meaning

Self-awareness brings better relationships.

behind these symbols, and your own reactions to the symbols, means you can identify with these qualities in your own life, work with them in a positive way and enhance personal development and relationships.

Symbols and archetypes have profound significance, with many layers and levels of meaning; they open us up to the hidden depths of ourselves which we might unconsciously choose to deny, repress or exile. This universal language makes the tarot a unique tool for self-understanding and for making choices about the future.

Self-understanding and psychological growth

The tarot provides an instant and direct way to understand the rhythms or patterns at work in your life. Uncannily, the tarot also seems to "predict" patterns or events that are about to happen. This may be our unconscious follow-up reaction based on the tarot's imagery at the reading.

We often want a signpost to a decision, or a confirmation of our doubts or belief in a relationship. The tarot can give us clues to the sort of day we might have, or whom we might fall in love with. Again, the cards reflect our own hidden desires, actions and goals. It can also help to develop our own self-awareness so that we can make conscious choices, understand the reasons behind a situation or give guidance as to the next stage of our personal life journey. In fact, the tarot is all about you.

An expression of any given moment

The tarot's potent use is to guide you, to make you draw on your intuitive senses, to "know" what it is you really want in life and to act upon that knowledge. The cards reveal the energy and mood that surround you, and give you insight into your self at any given moment, to open you to choice, and most of all to self-discovery.

The tarot is not evil

Tarot is not "spooky" nor is it "evil" unless the person who uses it chooses it to be so. The tarot is beyond our projection of good and bad and only reflects the energy of the moment and the reader. But we can project our goodness and badness onto it too. Using the tarot is a way to open yourself up to inner wisdom and hidden knowledge. Due to the Church's fear of anything esoteric that smacked of the occult, tarot became associated with the darker occultist arts, which is why people are often afraid of its power. Unfortunately, those collective associations still remain deeply embedded in our individual and collective psyches. Tarot is not intrinsically anti any belief or creed; it is simply a tool for revealing what *is*, in the truest sense.

A mirror to the self

Whatever the origins of the tarot (see page 16), it has inspired writers, poets and artists over the centuries. It

The tarot is like a mirror, providing an image of yourself at the time you look at it.

is a symbolic pathway you can walk along on at any moment in life to see the truth about yourself "through the looking-glass." It is simply a series of stepping-stones or secret pathways to self-discovery.

Past, present and future

Tarot cards are simply mirrors of our emotions, feelings, soul and being. They are like reflections on a pond where the visual images remain the same but vibrate with ripples caused by natural energies like the wind. Tarot moves with you, so that you can work with life, not against it. The tarot provides a mirror image of ourselves at the moment we choose to look at our reflection.

The history of tarot

The 78 cards of the tarot deck are made up of the Major Arcana and the Minor Arcana, which basically mean "big secrets" and "little secrets," respectively. Nobody really knows where the tarot originated; as with many mysteries, historians, writers and practicing occultists invented various historical roots colored by their own personal views.

But it is known that decks of mystical numbered cards existed in India and the Far East in ancient times and were probably brought to Europe by the Knights Templar during and after the crusades to the Holy Land. There have also been suggestions that traveling gypsies from the Far East brought the tarot to Europe during the Middle Ages.

Most sources believe the first tarot decks in Europe appeared in the early 14th century. These first decks seem to have arisen from a combination of early Italian four-suited playing cards and the set of 22 Major Arcana whose origin remains shrouded in myth and mystery.

The eighteenth-century French linguist, cleric, occultist and freemason Antoine Court de Gebelin was convinced of the mystical significance of the tarot. He claimed that the 22 Major Arcana was an ancient Egyptian book, or a set of tablets of mystical wisdom, remnants perhaps of the *Book of Thoth* (Egyptian god of mysteries and magic). Gebelin believed these mysterious tablets were brought to Europe by traveling *magi* (priests who followed the ancient Persian religion of Zoroastrianism) in early medieval time and were subsequently hidden away or lost. He devised his own deck using 77 cards, plus the Fool to make 78. The Major Arcana contained three times seven cards plus the Fool

The 16th-century magician John Dee used the tarot to talk to "angels."

Harding del.   Schenker sculp.

numbered zero, and each of the four suits of the Minor Arcana contained twice seven cards (ten pip cards and four court cards). His book, *The Primitive World, Analysed and Compared to the Modern World* volume viii, published in 1781, contained a chapter on the tarot and was accompanied by 78 designs that became the foundation for many later traditional decks.

Tarot imagery also has links with the "art of memory," a system of memorization invented by the Greeks to impress images on the mind for symbolic association. The Renaissance memory systems were subsequently linked to magical talismans and occult practices, and to magicians like the

Thoth was the Egyptian god of magic and words.

16th-century British astrologer and occultist John Dee, who took them one step further by using this system to talk to "angels."

No one really knows the origin of the word "tarot." Some sources suggest that it is a derivative of the name of the god Thoth, who was the Egyptian god of magic and words. Others believe it has Hebrew origins or is a corruption of the word "torah," the Hebrew book of law. And again some commentators believe it could be an anagram of *rota,* a Latin word meaning "wheel." Although not strictly an anagram, either the missing "t" or maybe a later addition of "t" provides yet another clue to solving the universal riddle hidden within itself.

Renaissance developments

Apart from its use as a mystical pathway, tarot was once used as a game in the Middle Ages known as *tarocchi* or *tarocchino* and later known as Trumps. It is still played as a game in Europe today.

The first cards were hand-painted, and one of the earliest decks is known as the *Visconti Sforza tarocchi* cards painted in the mid-1440s for the Duke of Milan. Other very early decks made up of 40 numbered cards and 22 Major Arcana include one belonging to Francois Fibba, an exiled Italian prince, and the *Mantegna* deck designed around 1470–85. These beautiful cards are very different from the deck we use now and examples exist in the British Museum.

The Mantegna deck is divided into five suits of ten cards each, and numbered from one to 50. The imagery expresses a universal order from the highest realms of the planets, down through the arts and the muses, and finally traditional imagery similar to the later standard tarot decks. Another well-known pack is the Marseille deck, which appeared at the end of the 15th century. Retaining the use of four suits of 14 cards, plus the Major Arcana, this deck has remained one of the most popular and distinct right up to the present day. Its imagery is dazzling and empowering.

The 19th-century revival

The 19th century saw an upsurge of interest in the occult, magic and esoteric mysticism. During this period the tarot spread from its adopted home in Europe to North America and to other parts of the world. Kabbalist and philosopher Eliphas Levi believed the source of the tarot was rooted in the sacred Enochian alphabet of the Hebrews. He also believed that the tarot did not necessarily predict, but it did reveal powerful knowledge to the wise. The social attitudes of the late 19th century created a biased distinction between divination and fortune-telling (which continues in some social circles today). Divination was apparently for the serious, intellectual elitist who coveted wisdom, while fortune-telling was considered a cheap way to make money by conning women and the lower classes.

Waite, Crowley and the Golden Dawn

Toward the end of the 19th century, Dr. Arthur Edward Waite developed and designed his own unique and radical tarot deck (later called the Rider-Waite deck) with the help of artist Pamela Coleman Smith. Waite was an initiate of the Hermetic Order of the Golden Dawn, one of the most influential occultist groups founded in 1888 by William Wynn Westcott, a doctor and master freemason, and by Samuel Mathers, a flamboyant character in Victorian British society. Drawing on many different esoteric beliefs, Mathers fused Egyptian

Dr. A.E. Waite radically changed the concept of tarot by designing his own deck.

magical systems with medieval magic texts and Eastern esoteric beliefs to create a workable magic system that also incorporated the Kaballah. In 1903, Waite took control of the Golden Dawn, and changed its name to the Holy Order of the Golden Dawn, to emphasize its more Christian associations.

The Universal tarot deck used in this book is still one of the most popular tarot decks in use today and integrates the original images of Waite's designs. Instead of the Minor Arcana being portrayed as mere playing card pips (clubs, spades, diamonds or hearts), he designed each card of the four suits as a symbolic image in itself.

In the 1940s British occultist Aleister Crowley designed the Thoth deck, together with Lady Frieda Harris. This controversial magus, notorious for his bizarre occult practices and heroin addiction, was also an initiate of the Order of the Golden Dawn, but was not liked by the other members. In 1907 he plundered the ideas of the Golden Dawn and formed his own order, the Silver Star, to include sexual and erotic magic. Crowley wrote many books on various occult practices and ideas, and in the 1960s there was a huge revival in his work. Intelligently written, his books form the beginnings of the first psychological approach to magic and occultism.

Crowley's deck embodies Egyptian, Greek, Christian and Eastern symbolism as well as many elements of other esoteric pathways. Crowley believed the tarot was an intelligence, a living force, and a key to the archetypal world within the self.

Since then, hundreds of tarot books and decks have been written and designed. The tarot has become more than just a fortune-telling tool; it is a comprehensive voyage of self-discovery, a mysterious and ancient symbol of all that we are.

Aleister Crowley, controversial occultist, designed his own deck in the 1940s.

Why use the tarot?

The tarot is an objective tool in the pursuit of self-analysis; the invaluable benefit of this kind of divination for self-awareness is that the cards never lie. Of course, the fortune-telling image of tarot still exists, and some of us really do want to "know" what our future holds. As long as we don't deny responsibility for our future choices by saying "the cards decided for me," then the tarot somehow, uncannily, seems to describe patterns of behavior. We are exactly what the tarot says we are.

The tarot is an invaluable tool for self-analysis and can help you to deal with difficult situations.

When you first start practicing with a "card for the day," you'll see how the card resonates to the energy, experiences and events of your day. The irony, of course, is that the tarot reflects the questioner's state of being and only mirrors back to you what you already are, both unconsciously and consciously.

Many people turn to the tarot for its archetypal and symbolic significance in their lives. It allows you the chance to truly develop your own choices and journey in life, and to bring greater awareness to your sense of purpose, destiny or vocation. Tarot is one of the most powerful tools for developing

With its rich imagery and symbolism, the tarot can easily be used for meditation.

self-awareness. It is timeless. Tarot inspires, creates pathways, gives guidance and makes a huge difference to the way you view your life and deal with its challenges. It is a wonderful tool for self-analysis and self-improvement.

Tarot not only brings fresh insight into making choices, and allows you to develop trust in your instincts and intuition, but it also opens up new horizons in relationships, career issues and personal fulfillment. By tapping into the energy of the moment, you are literally tapping your own psyche. It can also bring you closer to the spiritual and psychic side of your nature.

How it works

The word divination is derived from the Latin *divinus,* meaning "to be inspired by the gods." To "divine" is to foresee or foretell. Many cultures throughout the world and over the ages have "foretold" the future using anything from tossed twigs, coins and tea leaves to patterns in puddles after the rain. The desire to know what "will be" is a very strong human drive.

Coins used for I-Ching – another ancient divination technique.

But we seem to have lost the awareness that there is something "other," a connecting force that permeates all life and all existence. This connecting force includes the so-called "random" shuffling and choosing of the tarot cards. The belief that life is causal, that the only valid connection between two events is that one caused the other, is a modern scientific viewpoint. For example, "the car broke down because I didn't take it to the garage when I was supposed to." There is, however, a far more ancient and universal belief that everything in the universe is interconnected, and that events and patterns in the zodiac or the teacup, in another person's life or anywhere on Earth are all part of an invisible force. In other words, the randomness of divination is itself part of this process.

The great 20th-century Swiss psychologist Carl Jung coined the word "synchronicity" to describe such meaningful coincidences. He believed that the tarot card we select is prompted by something inner that needs to be expressed or must become manifest in the outer world at that moment.

The seemingly random choice of cards at any one moment is a powerful signifier of the meaning of that moment. It is almost as if the cards pick you, just as you pick the cards. We all project unconscious issues onto objects in the environment. We perceive reality through the tinted lens of our own nature. And we similarly project our inner issues onto each tarot card. Yet there is a message in every symbol and a meaning behind every image in the tarot. In return, the card awakens us to the powerful patterns in human nature that give us answers and solutions that we already unconsciously knew but didn't dare to believe possible.

The tarot works because it plays the chords that resonate in your soul. It is the music of your self.

Swiss psychologist Carl Jung developed the idea of synchronicity.

A symbolic language

The tarot is a symbolic language that draws on two symbolic sources: one is numbers, the other is images. These archetypal symbols trigger profound feelings within us and connect us to timeless myths and collective dreams. These ideas or deep-seated emotions need to be brought to life and carry within them many different layers of meaning for all of us.

Roses, for example, have always been associated with love, corn with fertility and arrows with spirited vitality. But roses have thorns and can hurt us in love; corn sheaves eventually become dry and brittle as our fertile creativity can "dry up." Take time to look closely at the symbolic images on every card, and, if you want to find out more about number symbolism, read the sections on numerology, astrology and the Kabbalah at the end of the book.

But where is this symbolic pathway leading us? Is it a learning curve or a divination method for making choices? The answer is that the tarot is both. Every card tells a story about our own personal journey at any given moment of time, and our interpretation and association with the symbols expands the tale. We read the tarot as if we were reading a book, but like any language it takes time to get to know it well. In fact, there are no precise or exact meanings for every card or layout, because the language of the tarot is wonderfully rich and changes with you.

Symbolic associations

Association is a key theme on the tarot journey. We do this in everyday language without thinking about it. The word "jug," for example, you'll immediately associate with a jug! But what kind of jug do you see in your mental or visual picture? Large, elliptical, long and narrow, squat, glass, ceramic, tin, colored, patterned or highly decorative? We each have a different perception of the word "jug," even though it is a common word. Once you start working with word associations you can see how important it is to work with symbols in this way, too.

So what about the word "tarot" itself? What associations do you make? Does it make you feel curious, wary, involved, fascinated, scared or enriched? Take time to think what you project onto that word and why it conjures up various associations for you. Make a list and play with the ideas to discover more about the way association works and your own feelings about the tarot.

A rose is a universal symbol of love.

Tarot as a mirror

The "mirror" analogy is the best one for understanding what you are actually doing when you read the tarot. Simply, you are reading you.

Look in a mirror, in water or in a shop window for a reflection of yourself. Obviously, you see yourself. But is it really you as others see you? Is your perception colored by what you want to see? The tarot, likewise, is a mirror. And your projections about love, life, hopes and fears are cast onto the cards as they are on the glass of the mirror. What you are actually reading in conjunction with the apparent random choice of cards are all those projections thrown back at you in a secret language, which you are going to learn to understand. As you begin to develop your ability to read the language of the cards, you also begin to connect to the archetypal themes and stories running through your own life with more objectivity.

Now try this exercise. Find a mirror. The one you use in the morning, or a beautifully framed antique mirror that adds glamor, mystique and charisma to the reflection it frames—you.

First of all, you will see your physical self and the usual things you like about yourself—your eyes, your hair, the perfect nose, the wry smile. Or you immediately notice the awful things like the bad hair, the pasty complexion, sagging chin, puffy eyes, a spot. Some us see the positive attributes, others see the negative simply because we are projecting "good" or "bad" onto what we see.

You might color your reflection with fantasies of who you might be. Or perhaps you camouflage your true features with other people's expectations of what is fashionable. Then again, you might be lucky enough to be objective and see through the color of your personal lens to the "real" you.

The tarot is an objective mirror. Of course you may still project onto the tarot cards your own issues, complexes or hopes and fears. But the irony is that you can now "see" what they are, revealed through the symbolic language of the tarot. Of course, sometimes you may not like what you see, but that's because the tarot is an objective mirror that always tells the truth.

The tarot reflects your hopes and fears each time you read the cards.

The deck and its structure

The tarot is made up of 22 cards called the Major Arcana, plus four suits of 14 cards called the Minor Arcana. The 22 Major Arcana represent profound archetypal qualities that permeate humanity, collectively and on an individual level. These qualities are represented by characters such as the Emperor, the Fool or the High Priestess, by several cosmic forces such as the Sun and the Moon, and by structures such as the Tower, the Wheel of Fortune and the Chariot. The other cards are the Magician, the Empress, the Hierophant, the Lovers, Strength, the Hermit, Justice, the Hanged Man, Death, Temperance, the Devil, the Star, Judgement and the World.

The 56 Minor Arcana represent events, people, behavior, ideas and activities that go on in our lives. When most of the cards in any layout are Major Arcana

The Major Arcana

The Fool   The Magician   The High Priestess   The Empress   The Emperor   The Hierophant

The Lovers   The Chariot   Strength   The Hermit   The Wheel of Fortune   Justice

cards, there is likely to be an important issue that needs attention in the life of the person concerned; the issue may still be unconscious, but is one that demands attention. If we choose a load of Minor Arcana cards, then it is likely that there is a very simple solution to a problem, or that events will unfold quickly. We know what needs to be done, or the events and experiences in our lives are simply showing us other aspects of what we are.

The four suits of the Minor Arcana are numbered Ace through to 10 of each suit, plus four court cards rather than the three associated with normal playing cards—King, Queen, Knight and Page (sometimes called the Knave). Note that some tarot decks also include a fifth court card called the Princess. The four suits are associated with the four elements: Swords with air; Wands with fire; Pentacles with earth; and Cups with water. As in the mirror exercise, think, feel, visualize and imagine how these associations work together.

| The Hanged Man | Death | Temperance | The Devil | The Tower | The Star |

| The Moon | The Sun | Judgment | The World |

The suits of the Minor Arcana

SUIT	ELEMENT	KEY WORDS
Swords	Air	Thought, information, connection, ideals, self-expression

SUIT	ELEMENT	KEY WORDS
Wands	Fire	Intuition, vision, progress, individuality, success, failure

SUIT	ELEMENT	KEY WORDS

Pentacles (Discs, Coins)   Earth   The senses, materialism, external reality, the tangible

Cups (Chalices)   Water   Emotions, feelings, relationships (love and sex)

Different tarot decks

These days you can find such a wide range of tarot decks, covering anything from gnomes to dragons, that it is quite hard knowing which is the best to use. My suggestion is to study as many as you can via the Internet and let your intuition decide which pictorial images say something to you. Below is a selection of traditional and more modern tarot decks that have been long-time favorites and are worth adding to any collection. For beginners I recommend the Universal deck used throughout this book, as well as the Rider-Waite deck upon which the Universal is based.

The Visconti-Sforza deck

One of the oldest known packs, originating from the end of the 15th century, it was created for the Visconti-Sforza family of Italy. More recently, additional cards have been added and painted to replace the original missing ones. This tarot deck is perhaps one of the most beautiful and enriched packs in existence, and has been recognized worldwide as one of the great examples of miniature art and Renaissance symbolism. The original deck included cards for Faith, Hope and Charity, and the Minor Arcana included an extra female knight and page per suit. However, none of the pip cards are pictorial.

The Moon from the Visconti-Sforza deck of cards.

The Sun from the Minchiate Etruria deck.

The Minchiate Etruria

The tarot, known in Tuscany as the *Minchiate*, was being used as early as the Renaissance in that region of Italy.

The Minchiate Etruria deck, produced in Florence around 1725, combines the more unusual pagan myths, the elements, the virtues and the signs of the zodiac. It has an odd structure, but it is fascinating in its rich imagery. Although the pip cards are not particularly pictorial, an odd satyr, unicorn or hedgehog appears when you least expect it.

The deck is made up of 97 cards. There are 41 Major Arcana cards, 19 of which appear in other decks, as well as the 12 signs of the zodiac and four virtues, plus, of course, the 56 suits cards.

The first 35 cards are called *papi*, and numbered with Roman numerals. They have no titles. The next five cards are called *arie* in the following order: the Star, the Moon, the Sun, the World and the Last Judgment (or Fame). The court cards are unnamed, too.

The Minchiate Etruria deck is illustrated throughout this book and is really worth adding to your collection once you understand the tarot better. The added elements of the astrological qualities and symbols can enrich and deepen your tarot reading.

The Tarot of Marseille

The Devil from the Marseille tarot.

There are several modern versions of the Marseille tarot, but they all originate from the deck first popularized in France in the 16th century and further developed by Claude Burdel around 1750. This is probably the most famous tarot deck of all, and has powerful, simple images in primary colors that evoke extraordinarily profound or hidden truths. Although crude, it is striking and effective; the fact that there are no pictures on the Minor Arcana cards can make them difficult to interpret. The older packs used Roman numerals, and later on usually bore the title of the Major Arcana cards in French, while continuing to use the Italian suits of Swords, Pentacles, Wands and Cups. This is a wonderful deck to use when you are more experienced.

The Rider-Waite deck

Dr. Arthur Edward Waite (1857–1942) was a serious scholar of all things occult, and believed that "the true tarot is symbolism." Under his strict supervision, Pamela Colman Smith, a fellow member of the Order of The

Golden Dawn, designed the 78 cards. This 19th-century British occult group, established by Samuel Mathers, William Woodman and William Wynn Westcott, attracted many prominent people of the time, including Waite, Edward Munch, August Strindberg, Rider Haggard, Aleister Crowley, William Butler Yeats, Bram Stoker and many others.

All the cards in this deck are completely pictorial, including the pip cards, and this precise imagery offers an immediate depth and accessibility to the meaning behind the cards. The pack was first issued in 1910, and since then

there have been various reissues and copies. The authentic Waite-Smith pack is known as the Rider-Waite deck and reproduces the true colors and images of the original. The deck used in this book, the Universal deck, sticks faithfully to the symbols, imagery and colors of the early pack.

The Crowley or Thoth tarot

Aleister Crowley, like many early 20th-century occultists, acquired a bad reputation. However, this charismatic, extraordinary man created a wonderful tarot deck that was

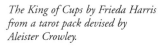

The King of Cups by Frieda Harris from a tarot pack devised by Aleister Crowley.

This watercolor of the King of Wands was painted for a tarot pack for Aleister Crowley.

designed and painted during the Second World War, just a few years before his death in 1947. The imagery reflects Crowley's eclectic occultist philosophy and, like the Rider-Waite pack, included both alchemical and astrological symbolism. Crowley worked closely with artist Frieda Harris to embed the secret teachings of the Order of the Golden Dawn (see page 21) into the card imagery, too.

The Thoth or Crowley tarot has become one of the most popular of the 20th-century tarot decks; the colors, imagery and geometrical symbolism make each card a work of art. The esoteric depth to these cards, however, can be more difficult to interpret. Crowley's pack differs from most decks in that he includes Knight, Prince, Princess and Queen, but no King. Each of the numbered Minor Arcana cards is titled with a key word. The Major Arcana is also radically different from the traditional decks with its 24 cards that include three Magus cards.

The IJJ tarot

The letters "JJ" refer to two cards, Juno and Jupiter, the Roman gods who were renamed "the Popess" and "the Pope" in later decks to keep the Church moderately happy. This deck is an old design that probably dates back to around 1670 and has been one of the most popular tarot packs in Europe and the United States. The images are very classical, with fine artwork, but the pip cards are not pictorial.

The Crystal tarot

This modern tarot deck, inspired by artist Gustav Klimt, was illustrated by Elisabetta Trevisan for Lo Scarabeo. Klimt was one of the great leaders of Art Nouveau at the end of the 19th century. This tarot deck contains mystical messages and is illustrated using tempera and pastels to create a delicate blend of colors and images; many of the images appear to have been painted as stained glass. The Crystal tarot invites you to enter a world of peace and harmony and evokes the qualities and archetypal messages of each card at its most potent and poignant.

Part 2

THE
tarot
directory

How to use the directory

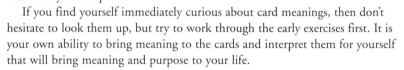

The nice thing about the tarot is that it is already
mapped out like a pathway. The steps along the
way are plotted for you. But, like any journey, there
are often hidden pitfalls and obstacles along the way. Take the
journey one step at a time, and if you are a beginner start with
the chapter entitled "Getting started" (pages 44–79). Practice
the exercises outlined in the chapter entitled "Developing
skills and knowledge" (pages 348–383), but also look at the
cards whenever you can and work with your own ideas, too.
If you are already familiar with the tarot, then you can start to
work immediately with the Major and Minor Arcana chapters
and the layout chapters.

If you find yourself immediately curious about card meanings, then don't
hesitate to look them up, but try to work through the early exercises first. It is
your own ability to bring meaning to the cards and interpret them for yourself
that will bring meaning and purpose to your life.

Interpretation chapters

In the chapters specifically set aside to discuss the individual meanings and
interpretations of each card, you will find phrases in the text such as "you
now," "blockage" and "future outcome" positions. These refer to the order in
which the cards were put down in some layouts. Many layouts use one of these
positions. "You now" is usually the first card laid down; the "blockage" card, or
your obstacles, is a card which crosses or sits at right angles on
top of another card. A "future outcome" card defines the next
step or stage of your journey.

However, there are layouts that don't have these specific
positions; in that case, work with each interpretation in depth.
Fundamentally, it's up to you to develop your own intuitive
interpretation based on the key symbols for the cards.

The Wheel of Fortune

ARCANUM 10
ZODIAC AFFINITY Jupiter

KEYWORDS
Inevitability, luck, timing, turning point, destiny

KEY PHRASES
- There is no certainty in life except uncertainty
- Each moment is a new beginning
- The only constancy is change itself
- Synchronicity and coincidence
- Seeing patterns and cycles repeating in life
- Feeling you are being swept along with the tide
- Taking advantage of chance
- Opportunity knocks, open the door
- Unpredictable events

Interpretation

The Wheel of Fortune is about luck and chance, but we can have good fortune and bad fortune – it is up to you to make choices that will lead to improving your sense of well-being or lifestyle. When you draw this card, the Wheel signifies that even though you are part of the greater cycle or universal or collective energies, destiny is about taking responsibility for your actions rather than blaming these actions on 'fate'.

If the Wheel of Fortune is a 'blockage' card, you might feel that your life is 'fated' and have no control over your feelings, experiences, love life or vocation. But it is that very lack of taking responsibility for who you are that is causing this problem. The Wheel says, 'Don't feel the world is against you, join in the cosmic dance and be part of the show, be your own choreographer.'

When in the 'yes now' position, the Wheel of Fortune signifies that you are ready to start afresh, turn over a new leaf or get ready for a great adventure. Whatever is happening, a new phase in your life is now beginning whether you want it now or not. Don't fear change, instead embrace it and take action for future happiness.

The Wheel can signify infatuation or a new romance, escaping from a difficult relationship or improving an existing one. It is time to jump on the bandwagon and take the chances that are coming your way. Unexpected events will give you the motivation to change your life for the better.

Five of Pentacles

KEYWORDS
Lack, victim mentality, hardship, rejection

KEY PHRASES
- Spiritual separation
- Soul-searching
- Emotionally wounded
- Unworthiness
- Feeling alone or excluded
- Neglecting your needs
- A sense that something is missing in your life

Interpretation

There is always a feeling of 'lack' when you draw the Five of Pentacles. It might simply feel like you lack material security on the surface, but there is something deeper at work here. There is a neediness, a feeling that something is missing, whether a spiritual connection or a meaning to life.

This card often appears when we feel emotionally deprived or have become a victim in a relationship. Sometimes it is easier and also more empowering to remain the deprived wanting person in a co-dependent relationship. This card also signifies that you are lonely, in need of love, feel unworthy of someone's love or are just neglecting yourself physically or emotionally.

The positive side of this card says that if there is something missing in your life right now, then you must go out and discover what it is. Perhaps you need a spiritual belief, more love, less materialistic dependency or more self-reliance. This is the mentality of someone who sees the glass half empty rather than half full, the pessimist who experiences a sense of rejection or abandonment. Feeling left out in the cold means that it is time to come into the warmth, but you have to take responsibility for doing so yourself.

If you fear asking for help, ask yourself why? Are you too proud, too fearful of opening old wounds, or are you denying your feelings at the expense of material benefit?

As a 'blockage' card, this indicates that you may be so wrapped up in your sense of deprivation that you can't see your way forward. The price to be paid for remaining a victim is that someone will always want to save you, but what kind of rescue do you really want? Isn't it better to rescue yourself? This card can also imply a fear (whether unfounded or not) of rejection, whether from a prospective employer, a publisher or lover.

Outer attitude, inner truth

This spread reveals your inner truth and the façade that we show to the world. The latter may not necessarily be in accord with your deeper feelings or intentions. Why not? Sometimes we fear that if we do what we really want deep down inside, we won't be loved. So maybe it is time to be more honest about what you want and be prepared to stand up for yourself. The cards that cross the inner truth cards represent the source of resistance (whether from within you or from a third party), or those things that are contrary to your inner intentions.

Attitude and truth spread

1 Inner truth about what you want
2 Outer attitude towards achievement
3 Inner truth about what you need
4 Outer attitude about values
5 Inner truth – your feelings
6 Outer attitude – reactions
7 Future inner truth to be revealed

Example reading

1 **The Magician** What you want deep down inside is to make an impact, to do something no one else has even dreamed of.
2 **Knight of Cups** But your outer attitude to achievement is unrealistic and often totally fanciful so no one really believes or trusts you.
3 **Strength** What you truly need is patience and self-determination.
4 **Nine of Cups** But you appear to value material gain over and above personal integrity.
5 **Three of Swords** Deep down you feel incredibly lonely, as if you are in emotional exile.
6 **Three of Wands** But you are good at covering this up with your ability to set an example or with your leadership skills.
7 **Seven of Swords** The inner truth revealed is that you must face the facts and stop running away from the truth. Don't deceive yourself.

There are also interpretations for every card in the Minor Arcana.

Easy-to-follow instructions for tarot spreads, plus example readings to help you interpret your cards.

How to use the directory

43

Getting started

First things first

If this is the first time you have thought about using the tarot, try to think about why you are using it. Why did you pick up this book? Are you curious, frightened, alarmed, excited? Is it because you generally want to know more about yourself, or to have some sense of control over your life? Is it to

Strength

be prepared for the unexpected or to help you answer a question that you already know the answer to but never dared admit? Or is it to access the inner archetypal world and "know" how your inner world interacts with external circumstances?

There are as many motivations for using the tarot as there are people. You must be aware of your personal agenda, and then with clarity and self-awareness you can take the first step in your individual tarot journey.

The Lovers

Pitfalls

There are a few things to watch out for as you embark on tarot reading:

- **Wanting quick answers or taking shortcuts in life.** Remember, issues may arise that need deeper work with the tarot, and it is always wise to develop your tarot skills before making any hasty judgments or assumptions.
- **Always interpreting each card the same way.** This is the most difficult habit to kick! It's easy to get stuck with one key word or interpretation because it's easy to remember. Liberate your imagination. Your life will flow better, too.
- **Being too subjective.** You might be projecting what you want to happen onto the cards rather than the truth. This is the most difficult aspect of tarot reading for yourself, because we always color what we see with who we are.

Potentials

Here are some of the things that tarot can do for you:

- **Teach you emotional honesty.** You will learn that with emotional honesty you become more willing to live life and make positive choices, rather than let it pass you by.
- **Develop your ability to focus and develop your own intuition.** Your intuition is there; you just need to let go of preconceived notions of how you should think and enjoy the interaction between you and your cards.
- **Develop your trust in the cards as your personal guides.** The more you practice, the more you will learn to trust.
- **Show you that the tarot is the most revealing mirror of you.**
- **Help you discover that you are able to take control of your life.**

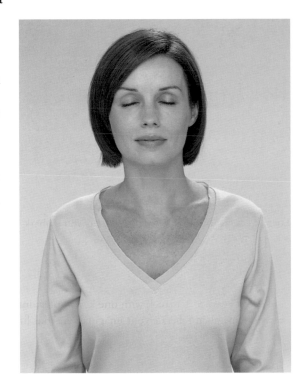

The tarot teaches you to trust your senses.

Choosing a deck

Nowadays there are hundreds of specialized tarot packs associated with anything from themes of Atlantis to rock-and-roll. It's all a question of personal taste. But whether you are a beginner or a serious tarot student, you need to get to know the archetypal symbols and language through which the tarot speaks. Opt for one of the traditional packs such as the Rider-Waite, the Universal as used in this book, or the Marseille or Mythic decks.

It is easy these days to find decks over the Internet, but to really get a feel for whether the cards suit you or, perhaps more importantly, whether you suit the cards, it's better to find a shop where you can handle some example cards as well as see them. When you harness the energy of any given moment, it's not just the sixth sense you need to acknowledge but the other five senses as well, so that all your senses are engaged in the moment to get you closer to what and who you really are.

*Specialized tarot images
from the Atlantis deck.*

Keep your tarot cards in a special place, such as a box or pouch.

Caring for your pack

There are no rules, but treat the cards as you would your true friends.

- When you first take the cards out of the box, lay them out on a clean table and allow them to "breathe"—exuding their energy and taking in yours.
- Connect with them. Touch them, pick them up, study them. Take your time.
- Each time you use them, either return them to their box or wrap a silk scarf around them as protection from rogue energies or harmful sunlight.
- If you do a reading for someone who has very negative energies or issues, perform a cleansing ritual after the reading.

Eventually, your cards will no longer be so new and pristine, and it's often the shabby old pack that you'll prefer for personal readings because it feels most trustworthy and holds so much of you within its substance. You may, of course, like to invest in more than one deck so that a brand new one can be brought out for special occasions or for readings for friends.

Getting to know the cards

The easiest and most traditional way to get to know the cards is to take one card for the day and study it. Create a story around it after reading its interpretation, and try to weave yourself into the plot. However, with 78 cards this method would take you 78 days. There is a quicker way.

Step-by-step guide

This kind of exercise will help you become familiar with all of the cards fairly quickly, giving you an impression, rather than in-depth knowledge. But it is a good place to start.

1 Separate the Major Arcana from the Minor Arcana, then lay the Major Arcana cards out in a line or in two rows, and decide if any "speak" to you. Does one card seem to resonate with your mood; do you feel it is trying to say something to you? Do you hate it, love it or fear it? Does it make you feel inspired, frustrated or sad?

2 Look up its complete interpretation to see whether it is relevant in any way to your life right now, or what is lacking.

3 Take out any cards that have this effect on you and get to know them first. One might be linked to your zodiac sign (see pages 356–363), or it just might be that you love the imagery and don't know why.

4 Look at the symbols on each card. Write down any that appeal to you—roses, lions, eagles, serpents, crowns—then try a little free association by writing down whatever comes into your head as you gaze at the image or symbol.

5 Keep a tarot journal of these thoughts and associations as you start to learn about the cards.

6 Next, work with the cards you don't particularly like or don't really understand. For example, some people can't identify with the Magician. Try to relate the card to your life now; is there a Magician in your midst? Do you have too many illusions? Or fear the unknown?

7 Getting to know the Minor Arcana is a little trickier. First read about what each suit represents and then learn about the court cards. You'll find the number cards' interpretations will follow quite naturally. Decide which suit you like best. Why?

8 Choose a court card; does it reflect you or a friend? Choose a number; is it meaningful for you right now? What does the image conjure up in your mind? Stretch your imagination—who are the kings and queens in your life, who are the pages and knights? Do you identify with their qualities?

Setting the scene

Whether you are a beginner or a more experienced tarot-card reader, before you start to do a reading make sure you are in a quiet, comfortable environment. This means you are able to focus and let your intuition flow rather than be distracted by passing cars, phone calls and other conversations. Once tarot reading becomes second nature to you, you'll find you can read the tarot anywhere. But make sure that you have enough space.

Initially you need enough space to lay out the cards—the floor or an empty table would be suitable. Don't attempt tarot readings in cluttered places, or you will find that you are distracted by the things around you. Finally, try to use the same place every time you do a reading, so that it becomes your sacred place.

Sit cross-legged on the floor. Light candles and incense or play soft music to soften your mood and allow you to focus. If you are reading for yourself, the more relaxed you are the better. Try focusing on a candle flame and meditate for a few minutes, then relax your breathing and try to drop all conscious thoughts.

Rituals

Many people like to use specific empowerment rituals before starting a reading. I always keep my tarot cards wrapped in a silk cloth. This protects the cards from negative

Incense will empower your tarot reading.

psychic energy as well as from natural elemental damage. You can create a protective magic circle, wear certain clothes or place items such as candles or crystals around you. These are all useful for getting the right energy flowing between you and the cards, and they help to put you in the right frame of mind. They also help with interpreting cards.

A pendulum can draw out negative energy.

Try the following:

• Choose your sacred place, unwrap your cards and light some incense. Sandalwood incense is good for psychic or healing powers, pine or rosemary for clarity of thought. Draw a circle of smoke in a clockwise direction over the tarot cards to empower them.

• Place one crystal in each direction—north, south, east and west— surrounding yourself. Choose your favorite crystals, but try to use same ones each time. This is your psychic space and the four elemental placements create a circle of protection. After you have finished your reading, uncast the circle by removing the crystals one by one in the same way you placed them—north, south, east and west.

Apart from the cards, candles, incense and crystals, you don't really need any other props. If you are doing a reading for someone else, you could pass a crystal pendulum over the cards to draw out any negative energies.

It is a good idea to keep a tarot journal. This is a great way of building up your knowledge. Your own insights and interpretations give you the key answer to any question, especially if you read back over your notes after the reading when you are more objective.

Shuffling techniques

The whole point of shuffling the cards is to make choosing them as random as possible. Tarot cards are larger than ordinary playing cards and do require a little dexterity if you want to shuffle them directly in your hands. There are very few hard-and-fast rules for shuffling, so do what is most natural for you. But always make sure you shuffle the cards face-side down.

Below are three different shuffling techniques that are simple and effective. Before you start shuffling, however, make sure that all the cards are in the upright position, in other words the pictures are facing you in the right direction. Don't turn the cards upside down while shuffling if you can possibly help it.

Technique one
Lay the cards face down on the floor or table. Spread them out wider and wider to make a long overlapping row, then gather some from the left and place them on top of those on the right. Then gather some from the middle and place them on top of the pile. Then gradually build up a pile of random cards. Do the whole procedure again and, finally, cut the pack at least three times to make sure they are well shuffled.

Technique two
When the cards are new they will be quite difficult to shuffle in your hands, but this is generally the preferred way. Try to drop cards that are in your dominant (writing) hand between other cards held loosely in the other hand. Even though they are large, you should be able to hold the complete deck in one hand. Keep shuffling until you feel the cards are well distributed. Then cut the pack three or more times to make certain that they are well shuffled.

Technique three

You can also shuffle the cards by spreading them out across the floor or table and simply stirring them round and round like mixing a cake. This means, of course, that some will probably be reversed, but when you lay them out you can simply turn them back to their upright position. Keep stirring them around and around in a clockwise direction first, then stir counterclockwise. Begin to gather them together in a group until you have a pile. Again, cut at least three times.

This is the best method of shuffling (technique two).

Drawing and choosing cards

The best way to choose cards for a layout, or just one card for the day ahead, is to fan them out in your hand and run your finger along the backs of the cards until one seems to "speak" to you. This isn't as easy as it sounds, especially if you have small hands. Do practice, but if you can't manage this technique lay the pack in front of you face down, then spread them out in an overlapping row of cards until you can see most of the edges.

If you are simply choosing a single card for the day, you can finish shuffling as normal, cut the pack three times, and either take the first card off the top or cut the pack and randomly select one from the center.

Choosing the card is the moment when you and the tarot merge. If you have a question or issue, focus on the subject or repeat the question to yourself while you draw each card.

In some ways, the tarot chooses you as much as you choose the tarot. You will probably find that one card shouts out for attention; other times you may be unsure if you've taken the right card or think you should have taken the one next to it. However, remember that if you hesitated to take a card and didn't choose it, it may imply that it wasn't meant to be taken by you on this particular occasion.

Once you have chosen one card for a layout, place it face up in its ordained position within that layout, and continue to choose subsequent cards in the same way.

Laying out the Celtic cross spread.

Letting go of projections

When drawing cards and placing them in a layout, it is important to let go of your projections as much as you can. (Projection can be defined as the unconscious ascription of a personal thought, feeling or impulse to somebody else, especially a thought or feeling considered undesirable.) We all consciously and unconsciously "project" our desires, wishes and fears onto the tarot, and emotional involvement with the question can often override the true response. So be very honest with yourself before asking questions.

The Death card represents new cycles beginning as well as old ones ending.

It is understandable to hope you'll get positive cards that affirm your feelings or give you the all clear to make headway with your plans. We all want to be empowered and feel that the future looks rosy. It is quite hard to look at a card like Death without feeling that something bad is going to happen. But there is no such thing as "good" and "bad" in the tarot; these are values we project onto each card. Good and bad are interwoven; they are inseparable. The tarot cards are neither good nor bad; rather they describe archetypal energies, influences and, of course, yourself. Use the information and try not to separate positive from negative when you see the images.

Embracing change

Although Death looks frightening, in its simplest form it represents the end of one cycle and the beginning of another, or the idea that change is inevitable. What you do with that knowledge is your choice. Think about the cycles that may be ending in your life now, even though you haven't drawn Death. There is always something beginning or ending. Think about what needs to be changed in your life to make it vivid and real.

Take the Death card from the pack now and study it. What emotions does it evoke? Do you fear change or welcome it in your life? If you are someone who hates change, then it might be unwelcome; in that case, maybe it's time to face that fear of change and turn it into something positive and creative.

Remember, the outcome of the reading is a projection of the moment you do the reading. It is up to you to make choices generated by that energy and make your future what you want it to be. Sometimes the cards merely confirm our feelings or gut instincts, and that is enough information to give you free rein to follow your desires. You know consciously or unconsciously what your current situation is about. The tarot enables you to recognize what needs to be done, said, not said or avoided.

The tarot is a mirror of you, it reflects the deepest part of yourself. Your shadowy side is brought out into the light of day, but how you interpret this is a mixture of traditional meaning and personal involvement. The only thing you can be sure of is that you might not see all there is to see.

What to ask

Sometimes you will have specific questions to ask. This is the easiest way to approach the tarot if you are a beginner, because you can generally use just one, two or three cards to get an answer. But avoid asking negative questions and particularly ones that mean you are denying responsibility for your choices. Example of questions that avoid responsibility:

You can improve your relationships by using the tarot.

- Will my ex-boyfriend/girlfriend come back to me?
- Should I change career?

Rephrase these questions as follows:

- I want my ex back, but how can I improve the relationship between us?
- A career change would improve my lifestyle. Can you help me find a way to decide what would suit me best?

Write it down

For specific questions, always write them down before you start shuffling or drawing cards. It is surprising how the question can be distorted when you merely think it in your head and, by the time you get to choosing a card or turning it over, you can easily twist the question to fit the cards. We all are capable of distorting the truth to suit us, because we all want positive results.

More often than not, you just want to get some "sense" of what is going to happen in the near future. There is usually an underlying motive for this "sense," so do try to focus on the issues and themes currently running through your life. Is there something uncertain or worrying about your current situation? Is it a relationship problem, career issue or does it arise from self-doubt? Keep a tarot diary to clarify these issues.

You might just want to use the tarot for self-development or to find out more about yourself or what themes are relevant in your life right now. Many of the spreads suggested in this book provide you with great insight into your personal journey. Often there are simply no questions to be asked (turn to page 76 for more information on reading for yourself).

It is helpful to keep a journal of questions asked and the results.

Intuition and association

After you have spent some time practicing, reading and interpreting the cards, you will begin to "know" intuitively what a card is saying. But, to begin with, you must get to know each card intimately so that they are all as familiar as your best friends. This requires time, effort and commitment on your part, but it's such an enjoyable experience that it won't seem like work.

Step-by-step guide

Many tarot books suggest inventing a story around the Major Arcana cards, using the Fool and his journey through each of the 21 other Major Arcana in order to get the know the cards. However, you can develop your intuition by forming your own associations for each card. Don't look at the interpretations for each card as you follow this simple exercise.

1 Sit in a quiet place, with nothing to distract you. Take the Fool from the pack. Gaze at the card in front of you and open your mind to the images you see. A youthful gigolo dressed in courtly medieval clothes. A cliff top or precipice, a dog barking at his heels, his head in the clouds, a rose in his hand, a stick and a bag. The sun is shining, there are mountains or clouds in the distance.

2 Now start your association chain of thought. Use all of your senses. Link colors, smells, sounds, taste, anything that comes to mind. For example, the youth's stance is carefree, he's not looking where he's going, and he's about to walk over the edge of the cliff oblivious to the dog frantically yapping a warning at his feet. He carries a rose; the cliff top is dangerous.

3 What do you associate with this card? The music could be a song like "Yellow Brick Road," the color could be yellow, the flower could be pansy or white rose, the sun is shining brightly—a solar image. Bright, lighthearted, pansy, yellow, "I'm off to See the Wizard of Oz."

4 Develop your own string of associations for each card and write them down. Then check your ideas with traditional associations to see how they match up. This will help you to use your intuition to read the cards and generate your own confidence about their meanings. You don't have to learn each card by rote, but do keep checking the interpretations and traditional associations as you start to read the cards more fluently. Like learning any foreign language, you have to practice to know it from the heart.

Your first reading

After you have become reasonably familiar with the deck and have spent some time familiarizing yourself with the cards, you can try a first reading.

Step-by-step guide

Use one of the layouts from the chapter on everyday spreads (see pages 254–275) for this practice reading. Remember, the images on the cards will evoke specific feelings within you personally, so, if reading the cards for yourself, analyze each card individually by using the chapters on the Major and Minor Arcanas (pages 80–253).

1 Prepare your environment, props and ritual. Make sure that you will not be disturbed for the period you have set aside.

2 Think about your question or theme, write it down, say it out loud as you shuffle and then lay out the cards in the order shown.

3 Focus on each card in turn and let your intuition guide you. If you feel you can't get the hang of what a card means, think about what you associate with that card. If you practice on a daily basis, you'll

soon get a sense of the most basic meanings. To begin with, don't worry if you can't get a feel for the card. Simply turn straight to the interpretations in the Major and Minor Arcanas chapters.

4 Look up the interpretation for each card. Read through all the key words and descriptions.

5 If you come across something that seems to really "fit" the situation, trust your intuition. Don't avoid interpreting cards you personally find unpleasant or

difficult to analyze. They probably mean more for you than you think.

6 If you are reading for another person take care that you don't project your emotional baggage onto the questioner. For example, you may immediately feel comfortable with the World (the card of self-fulfillment), associating it with travel, your favorite holiday or exotic locations. You might want to say, "hey, great, you're about to embark on a wonderful trip around the world." But the questioner might loathe travel, fear being away from home, and their sense of fulfillment might stem from family life and passive living. Bear this in mind when interpreting for other people, and don't forget, when reading for yourself, to keep a check on the traditional interpretations as you go along.

Develop your interpretation skills

The tarot cards symbolize various archetypes and qualities. These are neither good or bad; they just are. It is very important to remember this when doing any interpretation because it is human nature to judge qualities depending on their influence on us. We speak a language that splits the world into yes and no, good and bad, here and there, up and down. But this polarity is in itself part of the axis of "oneness," a "whole." By defining "here" we know that "there" exists; both are parts of the same polarity. We say "we are poles apart," but what are the poles if not the longitudinal axis of the world?

We all make judgments, mostly unconsciously, of what is "good" and "bad." However, a worthy aphorism to bear in mind when interpreting the cards is "One man's meat is another man's poison."

Finally, you will view these qualities from a different perspective depending on your current situation. For example, is being "generous" negative or positive? It all depends on your point of view at the time. Someone who is generous may well be buying your love; alternatively, they may be buying you more time.

Step-by-step guide

There are no rules to interpretation. Each person will read the cards differently. It takes practice, openness and willingness to learn and develop your skills and tarot language. But here is an easy exercise to get you started. Soon you will be able to read the tarot as if you were reading a book. The hard part is combining the interpretations of single cards in a layout. This is where you have to be a bit of a storyteller, and the easiest way is to say it all out loud.

1 Practice with two- or three-card spreads first to get you going. In the example shown below, the first card you choose represents your present situation, the second your recent past, the third the short-term future. Lay them out in this order:

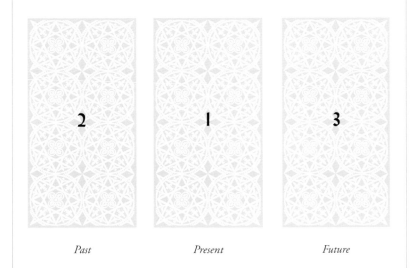

Past   *Present*   *Future*

2 Let's say that your question is "How can I improve my financial situation?"

3 For this example, let's assume that you choose the Star (present), Four of Wands (recent past) and the Heirophant (short-term future).

4 If you take just one of the main key words associated with each of these cards, you get inspiration, freedom, knowledge. Now try to relate these words to your question.

5 Next, think about personal associations you have with these cards. What do the images make you feel? Do the words suggest "bad" or "good" qualities to you? You might be someone who hates convention, and the fear of having to stick to the rules means the Hierophant (whose key words include conforming, traditional rules, respect) is more threatening than helpful. But it is, in fact, via the system and the people who represent it that you will get a positive outcome.

6 A very simple interpretation of these cards would be: "right now I'm *inspired* to do something about my finances, in the recent past I've been spending too *freely*, but in the future I'm going to have to listen to *conventional* financial advice to improve my situation."

Example reading

1 The Star (key word: inspiration) You are inspired to
do something about your finances, but on reading about
the Star in detail you realize this isn't a practical card.
However, you have enough motivation now to sort out your finances.

2 Four of Wands (key word: freedom) Recently you've been spending
money freely, perhaps celebrating too much or simply enjoying the good life.
But being overly generous has left your wallet empty (in this case the word
generous isn't exactly "good").

3 The Hierophant (key word: conventional knowledge) The key to good
finances is to listen to someone who can advise you. It is with knowledge,
conventional though it is, that you can make headway.

Try this method with different questions and different cards to practice using
simple key word interpretations first.

2

1

3

Yes or no answers

Sometimes you may want to ask a simple question that requires a simple yes or no response to determine your future. But remember that most of the cards carry both positive and negative associations, so try to analyze what the underlying motives for your question are before interpreting one card for a yes/no answer.

However, there are a few cards which appear to be particularly positive and

others particularly negative. The Devil could easily be taken to signify a "no," and the World a "yes." It all depends on the question, since even "no" answers can be positive. You may be eagerly hoping for a "yes" response when you ask questions like "will he/she marry me?"; "will I get the job?" You might be asking a question to determine someone's feelings: "does my partner love me?"; "is my colleague a rival?" The answer "no" to the last question would be a positive response because it shows that your fear is ungrounded.

But remember that yes or no answers aren't very revealing. There are so many other options involved in any question. Even if you simply want to know if your partner loves you, it would be more revealing for you to discover more about their feelings through a in-depth relationship spread.

Three-card yes/no trick

You can use the upright or reversed positions of three cards to determine a yes or no answer. For this you will need to shuffle the cards and make sure that some of the cards turn upside down randomly as you shuffle. Next, choose three random cards and lay them face up in a line. Upright cards count as yes, and reversed cards count as no. Obviously if you have two "yes" cards and one "no" card, then the answer is yes to your question, and so on.

yes   *no*   *yes*

Two uprights and one reversed card equals "yes."

Drawing a daily card

Another good way to develop your interpretation skills is to draw a card for the day. If you are a complete beginner, then work with the Major Arcana on their own first, so you really get a feel for their archetypal symbols. Throughout the day you should think about the card, freely associate the ideas, check its various interpretations and see it how it works for you during the day. At the end of the day make a note of the card and what issues arose for you. Did the card correspond to the energy of the day, the people you encountered, your feelings or your actions? Write down any events, encounters, ideas or experiences that relate to the card you choose.

Step-by-step guide
Make your card for the day a daily ritual, just like any other—brushing your teeth, making tea or coffee, getting dressed. All you need is a couple of minutes and it will prepare you for a fresh outlook on your day.

1 Find a quiet time, maybe just on waking. Shuffle the pack, cut as many times as you like and empty your mind of all thoughts. You do not have a question in mind, since you are randomly picking a card as your day's adviser.

2 Fan the cards out in one hand face down and choose one card from the pack, or alternatively take one from the middle, center or top of the pile.

3 If the image happens to be upside down, don't interpret it this way, but simply flip it to its upright position.

4 Before you look up the card's key words and interpretations, take your time to develop your own

thoughts and feelings about what it means to you. Have you already an idea in your mind of what it symbolizes? For example, you pick the Hermit, a card of introspection. You might imagine that you are going to feel lonely all day. You might in fact do so, but the Hermit also indicates that you need to look back; perhaps you'll encounter someone from your past who says something meaningful to you. You should ask for advice from someone you trust or set off on some personal quest.

5 Let the interpretation guide you, but often a sudden revelation, an encounter or an experience will allow you to see what the card means to you, and its relevance in your life that day.

Reversed cards

There are many different opinions and a longstanding debate within tarot circles about the meaning, relevance or otherwise of reversed cards. It is all a matter of personal choice whether you heed them or not.

When doing a reading, if you prefer not to use reversed cards, simply shuffle them so that the cards are always in the upright position. Alternatively, as you lay out the cards in a spread, turn them round so the upright position faces you. This is simply a matter of personal choice.

Tarot cards symbolize archetypal energy, and when you do a reading you form a relationship with that energy; your actions, feelings and intentions are synchronized to that moment. The tarot reveals the archetypal energy that currently reflects your situation.

But what do reversed cards signify? Traditionally it was thought they simply represented the opposite of the upright card and were usually given negative connotations. But this is confusing, because the symbolism of the upright card conveys the message, both negative and positive.

Others say that an upside down card reveals that the energy is there, but not yet developed. The potential has been seeded, but the energy to be expressed is currently dormant; or it may be moving away from you, or is simply unavailable to you right now.

Using reversed cards

If you want to use reversed cards, the simplest way to interpret them is to consider that this quality may be somehow lacking in your life right now, or that the qualities it represents need to be made conscious. You might need to pay more attention to that card and its full meaning.

Personally, I always turn all cards into the upright position, because the rich symbolism of the upright cards will tell you what is lacking, what is needed, which energy is passive, dormant or active at any moment in your life.

Take the Moon, for example. The upright Moon represents confusion, illusion and self-deception. It also represents imagination, intuition and time to

Whether upright or reversed, the Moon has similar meaning.

discover your true way forward. If it was reversed, would this really change anything, as the Moon embodies both "negative" and "positive" qualities? Perhaps the only extra benefit gained from using the reversed position is to say that you need to be more conscious of self-deception or pay more attention to intuition. But the same could be said if the card fell in an upright way in a key position in one of the many example layouts.

Reading for yourself

There are times when you can use the tarot for self-development, to open yourself up to psychological, spiritual or soul-searching issues that might be locked away in your unconscious. You can also use this method when you feel

The tarot gives positive guidance for life-changing improvements.

the future is a big unknown factor and you want some direction. Reading for yourself is useful if you are standing on the threshold of a new relationship, new career or big life change and need a sense of the larger patterns and energies at work in your life. This is when you don't need to ask any questions, but simply trust in what the tarot will reveal to you.

Step-by-step guide

Rather like drawing a card for the day, this kind of reading requires no careful approach to questions. You don't have to write anything down, nor even say things aloud. In some way the deeper implications of the tarot's mirroring effect will work by showing you the bigger picture and the important themes being generated.

1 Empty your mind of mundane thoughts, relax and begin to shuffle the cards. While doing so, don't focus on anything, just let your thoughts blow through you rather than attach yourself to anything specific.

2 Use one of the layouts described on pages 254–347 to guide you. But once you become more familiar with the cards you can create your own layouts for this kind of inner work.

3 Look at the themes that the combined cards evoke, but don't try to analyze them in detail. Allow your unconscious to work directly with the energy, and as you gaze at the cards you will begin to understand the themes or issues that are currently important for your future.

Reading for others

Although this book is aimed very much at personal tarot work, there will be times when you'll want to read cards for other people. This requires a little more psychological awareness and care.

We all project our ideas, feelings and issues onto the qualities represented by the cards. What is "great" for you might be "boring" or "unthinkable" for someone else. You may think the Tower card is exciting and dynamic, because it suggests sudden changes or surprise events and you personally thrive on that kind of spontaneity. However, someone else might get their kicks by being in control and find that idea threatening rather than liberating.

Try to be very objective when reading the tarot for friends.

When you start reading for others, always make it a fun experience, and accept that you will probably learn more about yourself by reading the tarot from a more objective viewpoint.

But do take care with friends. Before you begin, ask yourself if you are emotionally involved, do you have a vested interest in their situation, do you want something good to happen to them? The art is to remember that you are seeing the situation from your viewpoint, so try to be as objective as possible. Also, interpret the cards in relation to the question without falling into the trap of twisting things around because the friend wants to hear this, that or the other, rather than the truth.

Reading for absent friends

You can lay out the cards and ask a question pertaining to someone who isn't present. This can be good fun or fraught with projection. Again, reading on behalf of someone else or about a mundane situation requires complete emotional honesty. Personally, it's amusing to ask questions like "what is my lover thinking about me right now?" or "when I meet my great-aunt next week for tea, how is it best to deal with her?" or "if the blah blah party win the election how will it affect my family?"

Steer away from questions like "why does A hate B?," or "will Jane split up with her current boyfriend?" since these issues are really no one's business but the people concerned.

You can read the tarot with your partner for fun as well as for future insights.

The
Major
Arcana

Understanding the Major Arcana

The Major Arcana, meaning "great or big secrets," represent the most fundamental energies of life. The cards symbolize our most basic issues, our inner world and underlying motivations. These are the 22 qualities or archetypes that permeate all mankind, and they draw out deep and complex reactions in us all. Think about whether you are spooked by "Death," allured by "the Lovers," indifferent to "Temperance," angered by "the Devil." We all carry these archetypes within us. If you can avoid projecting negative or positive values onto the cards, their rich symbolism will provide you with greater self-knowledge as well as guidance on how to take responsibility for your own destiny. These cards represent you.

Checklist

The 22 Major Arcana represent deep archetypal influences and qualities at work in both the individual and the society at large, but the cards also express unconscious and conscious psychological aspects of yourself. For each card within this chapter you will find the following information:

- Each card has a name. Some are simply ideas or themes such as Temperance, Judgement and Strength, while others are individuals who personify a particular quality such as the Hierophant or the Magician. The Moon, Sun and Star represent deeper, more esoteric unconscious forces.
- Each card has a number known as the Arcanum. The Major Arcana are numbered 1 through 21, plus the Fool who has no number, but is sometimes referred to as 0.
- Each of the Major Arcana interpretations is accompanied by astrological and numerical correspondences.
- Each card has key words and phrases to help you identify the main theme or "feel" of the card. These brief phrases describe how the energy of the card is manifest. For example, the Fool's key words suggest "going on a personal quest," "impulsively heading off into the unknown."
- Each card has a main interpretation, which describes the card in detail and gives more information about possible interpretations when placed in various key positions in spreads (see pages 254–347 for examples of spreads).

Key positions in spreads
- "You now" position describes the current situation
- "Future outcome" position describes the future situation
- "Recent past" position describes recent influences on the issue
- "Blockage" position describes current obstacle

The Fool

ARCANUM 0
ZODIAC AFFINITY Uranus

KEY WORDS

Impulse, infatuation, blind to the truth, childlike, pure and uncorrupt

KEY PHRASES

- *The eternal optimist*
- *Ready to leap into anything*
- *Taking each adventure as it comes*
- *Spontaneous and carefree*
- *Going on a personal quest*
- *Impulsively setting off into the unknown*

Interpretation

The Fool usually implies new beginnings and childlike enthusiasm for life. This card represents the part of yourself that comes to life when you need adventure, fall in love or are looking for quick answers; the inner child or crazy fool who acts without thinking, unafraid of the unknown and ready to leap in at the deep end.

The Fool always signifies the unpredictable, that life is full of surprises and that anything goes. It can indicate that it is time to let go of worries and self-doubt, to take a leap of faith rather than fear making a choice.

In a relationship issue, watch out for falling in love with love and not looking where a relationship is heading. This card can also imply you have an immature attitude toward relationships or your professional abilities. Perhaps you are avoiding responsibility.

The Fool can mean that you won't listen to anyone's advice and that you are being careless with promises and feelings. You may be blind to future heartaches or rush into a new venture too soon without thinking things through. The main feeling behind this card is a warning to look before you leap, but if you are confused about making a decision the Fool implies that it's time to believe in yourself and trust your heart. Sometimes resistance is more foolish than risk.

If the Fool appears in a "future outcome" position, then it can signal a new beginning or change of direction. Perhaps an irresponsible, wild, uninhibited lover, friend or stranger will become important in your life. In any question concerned with sexual intimacy, the Fool represents erotic vitality, *joie de vivre*, but also a reluctance to make any commitments.

The Magician

ARCANUM I
ZODIAC AFFINITY Mercury

KEY WORDS

Initiative, persuasion, conscious awareness, action

KEY PHRASES

- *Ability to manifest*
- *Realizing your potential*
- *Knowledge is the key to success, but don't deceive yourself that you know all the answers*
- *Focusing on a goal*

Interpretation

The Magician is the archetypal achiever. He taps into all the universal forces to get results.

The Magician symbolizes the bridging effect between the inner and outer you, how your unconscious desires filter through to your conscious and make things happen. When you draw this card it is important to be flexible, to communicate, to listen to your inner voice. You might also have to guide a friend or partner toward making the right choice for them. Persuasion is your ally, so set the pace and inspire others with your ideas. This is a "go out and get it" card.

The Magician also represents your ability to make choices and to confidently work with your skills and knowledge as long as you don't think you have the answer to everything. This is a highly creative card in relationship issue layouts, and can signify masculine sexual energy. In business matters it can indicate you are the ultimate high achiever, have a knack for producing seemingly magical results or for turning a situation around that others couldn't see how to resolve.

If this card appears in a "you now" position, then it is timely to adapt to changing circumstances, juggle with ideas and find the right way forward.

As a "future" card, it reveals that you will soon have to prove you can communicate effectively.

In the "blockage" position, this card often indicates that you are so focused on yourself that you are ignoring your deeper needs and values. Perhaps you need to acknowledge your true intentions, or practice what you preach.

The High Priestess

ARCANUM 2
ZODIAC AFFINITY Moon

KEY WORDS

Secrets, hidden feelings, intuition, the healer, feminine power, silent potential, the unconscious, hidden motivation, mysterious influences, developing talents

KEY PHRASES

- *A secret needs to be revealed*
- *Trust in your intuition*
- *Seeing beyond what is obvious*
- *Remembering something of significance*

Interpretation

The High Priestess is the archetypal symbol of all that is unknown. She is all-seeing, but gives nothing away and guards the secrets of the unconscious. She represents the interface between the apparent real world and all other realms. When you draw this card it is timely to look behind the veil of life's illusion, to look beyond that which is obvious or plain fact, and to accept that there is mystery in life, too.

In the "you now" position, the High Priestess indicates that you need to unlock your memory box, develop your hidden potential or listen to your intuition to guide you. This card represents feminine power but, unlike the Empress who represents worldliness, the Priestess symbolizes the esoteric unknown factor, the feminine instinct that has mystified mankind for thousands of years.

In the "blockage" position, this card reveals that you fear finding out how you really feel about someone, but that it is also time to develop your awareness and use your intuition about what you really want and where you are going. There are many secrets in your heart, and if you look within you'll find the truth. Maybe you are finding it hard to communicate your feelings to someone.

As an "outcome" card, you will soon be enlightened about a problem or a secret will be revealed. As a "past" card, think back to what someone said to you a few days ago; it could be revealing or lead you to the answer you have been seeking. A remembered conversation will bring you success.

The Empress

ARCANUM 3
ZODIAC AFFINITY Venus

KEY WORDS

Action, development, feminine vitality, sensual pleasure, abundance, compassion, creativity, nurturing, feeling good about life

KEY PHRASES

- *Focusing on beauty and art*
- *In harmony with the natural world*
- *Being extravagant*
- *Luxurious living*
- *Sensual awareness*

Interpretation

The Empress represents the creative, nurturing aspect of the feminine. Her archetype is one of abundance, fertility and creativity. This card is concerned with nature, the arts, grace, beauty and, at its worst, greed, possessiveness and overindulgence.

When you draw this card in a "you now" position, it can indicate your nurturing instinct is powerful and you need to concentrate on creating harmony in your relationships. Alternatively, perhaps you need to nurture your own heart or get in touch with your sexual needs.

This card can indicate you are in the process of mothering someone or about to become a mother. But it can also suggest a mother figure is going to be an important influence in your life.

If you draw this card in a "future outcome" position, you can be assured of progress in any plan, however daunting it may seem.

If you have asked a question about relationships, the Empress indicates you might have to motivate your partner or mother them. It can also suggest that there is a disruptive female influence in your life, especially if in the "blockage" position. This could be someone at work or your mother.

Material wealth or property will be important to you in a "future" position, but it is also time to be creative with your life rather than assume things will just fall into your lap. The Empress reveals that you must be aware of your instinctive nature as well as the rational.

The Emperor

ARCANUM 4
ZODIAC AFFINITY Aries

KEY WORDS

Power, authority, father-figure, leadership, the power of reason

KEY PHRASES

- *Insensitivity to others, to their feelings and passions*
- *Assertive dogmatic thinking*
- *Orderly chaos*
- *Establishing laws or family values*
- *Taking control of a situation*
- *Structured thought*
- *Sticking to the rules*

Interpretation

This card represents the masculine principle, the archetype of authority, fatherhood and leadership. When your inner Emperor is activated, you are ambitious and can manage your affairs efficiently. When you draw this card in a "you now" position, you have authority and know what you want, but maybe you are too forceful and stubborn, always wanting everything your own way.

In a question concerning partnership, it signifies that you have the will and the need to take control of the relationship. But it's time to keep personal feelings out of the firing line, and base your decisions on pure fact. As a "blockage" card, the Emperor reveals that someone in authority is preventing you from moving on, or that a lover or father figure won't listen to what you have to say.

If you are asking a love-related question, and this appears as a "future" card, the Emperor means you will be attracted to a strong, dominating person or a successful career go-getter. Power trippers and cold-hearted lovers are also signified—they may be reliable in bed or around the office, but you'll never know their true motives. If you are trying to find out about a vocational issue, this card suggests that through self-discipline and determination you will achieve your ambitions or goals.

The Emperor reminds you that structure, organization and the rulebook will get you the best results.

The Hierophant

ARCANUM 5
ZODIAC AFFINITY Taurus

KEY WORDS

Conforming, holding back, respect, teaching, traditional rules and ceremony

KEY PHRASES

- *Fitting in with the status quo*
- *Accepting discipline*
- *Peer pressure*
- *Studying higher values*
- *Sharing a belief system*
- *Knowing how to act appropriately*
- *Discrimination from knowledge*

Interpretation

The archetype of the Hierophant represents knowledge and education in its most accepted form. When you draw this card it indicates that traditional values are appropriate for any action, but also that your inner spiritual soul needs expression.

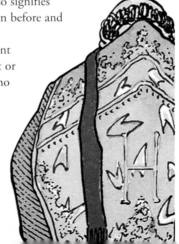

If you are asking a relationship question, the Hierophant signifies that someone is acting in a conventional way or that you must seek out the guidance of someone who acts as a guru or mediator. It can also indicate that you must conform to certain rules if you are to move ahead with your plans.

If the Hierophant is drawn in a "you now" position, you may be stuck in your ways and are unwilling to adapt to others. Clinging to the past means that you can't move on and accept the necessary changes that will improve your life.

In the "future" position, the Hierophant often represents a specific person you will meet—a guru, spiritual adviser or teacher who has good advice and should be trusted. It also signifies meeting with someone you feel you've known before and with whom you have an immediate rapport.

The most important lesson the Hierophant teaches is that, however much you may trust or stick to your own beliefs, there are others who have their own too. You may be battling against restrictions imposed by others or perhaps circumstances, or an orthodox group of people is limiting the free-spirited, independent side of your nature.

The Lovers

ARCANUM 6
ZODIAC AFFINITY Gemini

KEY WORDS

Love, completeness, choice, temptation, commitment

KEY PHRASES

- *The power of love and how we deal with it*
- *What do you mean by the word "love"?*
- *Seeking wholeness*
- *Being true to your values*
- *Sexual harmony*
- *"Made in heaven" relationship*
- *Romantic desire*
- *Feeling drawn to another*
- *Making a choice*
- *Knowing what is right and wrong for you personally*
- *Wanting union*

Interpretation

The Lovers is a card everyone wants to draw, but it is far more complex than just signifying new love in your life, or harmony and happiness. The image reveals that we are all separate individuals, however close we feel to someone sexually or emotionally, and we must acknowledge each other's personal values or needs.

If you draw this card in the "you now" position, your heart rules your head or you want to be in love and escape the doubts, fears and inhibitions of the world around you. If you draw this card as a "future" card, new romance could come into your life without you even looking for it.

This card also implies that it is time to make a relationship choice. Do you commit? Will your partner commit? Do you go your own ways? Conflicts can be resolved if this card is in the "future" position, but can also indicate that temptation will test the strength of a current relationship. Love triangles are also signified if this card appears in a "future" position. You may have to choose between two people or may even be tempted to get involved with someone who is already in a long-term relationship.

The Lovers archetype also asks you to think about what you, personally, mean by love and to take responsibility for your choices. We all use the word "love" very glibly, but love is different things to different people. You may want unconditional love, whereas someone else may want conditional love, approval, or be seeking to manipulate others to feel loved. This card asks you to be more aware of who you are and what values you place on love relationships.

The Chariot

ARCANUM 7
ZODIAC AFFINITY Cancer

KEY WORDS
Diligence, willpower, honesty, perseverance

KEY PHRASES
- *Control over feelings and thoughts*
- *Being pulled in two directions*
- *Learning to stick to the right path*
- *Sexual prowess*
- *Being successful*
- *Determination to win at all costs*
- *Wanting victory*
- *High adventure and taking risks*
- *Being in the driving seat*
- *Mental and physical journeys*

Interpretation

The Chariot reveals that strong motivation and self-will are the key to progress, particularly if it is placed in the "you now" position. This card is all about confidence, healthy ego and self-belief. Either you will have the self-assurance and spirit to get what you want, or you will meet someone who represents this archetypal force in your life. They may not be particularly likeable, but they get results. They mean business.

Alternatively, the Chariot can signify that there may be conflicting influences in your life. You have now reached a point where you can stand up for your own beliefs and make decisions based on what you want rather than what other people assume is right for you.

You will achieve success in any enterprise and overcome all obstacles in your way. As a "future" card, timing and control are essential to get what you want, so don't let the reins slip through your fingers; stay on top. Maybe your relationship needs reevaluating. Whatever your mission, only you can make it work. It is time to crack the whip.

The Chariot can also mean that self-control or an outside controlling force will help you achieve your goals. There is also a need to be competitive when you draw this card in the "future outcome" position. It's up to you to take control of your life and beat any rivals in your camp. You can master your emotions, concentrate your energy and get your own way, so trust in your own integrity and you will progress.

In the "blockage" position, the Chariot implies that you are too controlling or that you are being hampered by someone who only thinks of themselves and won't let you take hold of the reins.

Strength

ARCANUM 8
ZODIAC AFFINITY Leo

KEY WORDS

Strength, courage, self-awareness, compassion

KEY PHRASES

- *Facing reality*
- *Taking control of your life*
- *Learning to take responsibility for your actions*
- *Ability to forgive imperfection*
- *Being tolerant of others' faults*
- *Inner strength*
- *Awareness of your instinctive responses*

Interpretation

Strength and the courage of your convictions are needed in the "you now" position. Be prepared to face any threat with determination. It is time to force the issue to achieve results. However, it is not so much physical strength that is required here, but mental and emotional strength expressed through compassion rather than the self-willed "Look at me!" energy of the Chariot.

When you draw this card, you must also be prepared to forgive and forget or to accept someone needs more space or that you can't always have your cake and eat it. It's timely to take a calm approach toward others' anger or your own. Are you feeling frustrated? Do you feel out of control of a situation and therefore also feel vulnerable yourself?

If you are asking a question concerning love or romance, think about whether you are giving too much of yourself or not getting anything back from a partner. If in a "future" position, self-awareness and tolerance of others' faults will bring you success. You will soon have the inner strength and stamina to get through any prickly hedges. If other people are driving you mad, don't forget that it's your compassion, your ability to see both sides of the argument, which will get you results. Gentle guidance may be needed to resolve a love problem, but most of all understanding your own underlying motives and emotional responses will get you through any current difficulties.

The Hermit

ARCANUM 9
ZODIAC AFFINITY Virgo

KEY WORDS
Discrimination, discretion, detachment, withdrawal

KEY PHRASES
- *Search for inner wisdom*
- *Knowledge is a burden*
- *Fear of revealing a secret*
- *Needing the truth at all costs*
- *Wanting to be alone*
- *Self-searching questions*
- *Looking for direction or guidance*
- *Withdrawal from relationship*

Interpretation

The Hermit represents the most secretive part of ourselves. When you draw the Hermit as a "you now" card, it reflects your need to look within for answers, to do some soul-searching or to take a break from the rat race or other people's opinions and formulate your own. This card also signifies that it's time to reflect carefully before you make a choice and avoid rushing ahead with plans that could push others into doing something against their judgment.

If you are seeking guidance for a relationship issue, think long and hard before committing yourself to any long-term plans. Take a step backward, look at the patterns of behavior, emotions and feelings in any past relationships to give you insight into whether you are taking the right pathway.

As a "past" card, you may have chosen to forget certain facts or are refusing to face up to the truth. As a "future" card, you will have to put your plans on hold until you can discriminate between what is right for you and what isn't. As a "blockage" card, it's your personal sense of isolation or loneliness that is holding you back.

The Hermit also signifies that inner healing may be needed in order to create a more emotionally balanced way of looking at life. Look to your inner guide, whether a spiritual belief, deity or simply a guardian angel—whatever you put your trust and faith in will guide you out of any darkness and into the light. The Hermit stands for stillness, for calm, for guidance, and you may need to seek advice from an older friend, family member or wise mentor.

The Wheel of Fortune

ARCANUM 10
ZODIAC AFFINITY Jupiter

KEY WORDS

Inevitability, luck, timing, turning point, destiny

KEY PHRASES

* *There is no certainty in life except uncertainty*
* *Each moment is a new beginning*
* *The only constancy is change itself*
* *Synchronicity and coincidence*
* *Seeing patterns and cycles repeating in life*
* *Feeling you are being swept along with the tide*
* *Taking advantage of chance*
* *Opportunity knocks, open the door*
* *Unpredictable events*

Interpretation

The Wheel of Fortune is about luck and chance, but we can have good fortune and bad fortune—it is up to you to make choices that will lead to improving your sense of well-being or lifestyle. When you draw this card, the Wheel signifies that, even though you are part of the greater cycle or universal or collective energies, destiny is about taking responsibility for your actions rather than blaming those actions on "fate."

If the Wheel of Fortune is a "blockage" card, you might feel that your life is "fated" and have no control over your feelings, experiences, love life or vocation. But it is that very lack of taking responsibility for who you are that is causing the problem. The Wheel says: "Don't feel the world is against you, join in the cosmic dance and be part of the show, be your own choreographer."

When in the "you now" position, the Wheel of Fortune signifies that you are ready to start afresh, turn over a new leaf or get ready for a great adventure. Whatever is happening, a new phase in your life is now beginning whether you want it to or not. Don't fear change, instead embrace it and take action for future happiness.

The Wheel can signify infatuation or a new romance, escaping from a difficult relationship or improving an existing one. It is time to jump on the bandwagon and take the chances that are coming your way. Unexpected events will give you the motivation to change your life for the better.

Justice

ARCANUM 11
ZODIAC AFFINITY Libra

KEY WORDS

Fairness, harmony, equality, cause and effect

KEY PHRASES

- *Objective thinking restores balance*
- *Interaction and communication are essential*
- *Accepting the truth*
- *Taking responsibility for your choices*
- *Making decisions*
- *Looking at both sides of the argument*
- *Sexual equality*

Interpretation

What is fair to one person may not be so to another, but when you draw this card you are being reminded to take a very rational view of the situation or issue at stake. How involved are you emotionally? Can you see the wood for the trees or do you believe that someone else is being unfair or judgmental? Justice asks us to look logically and objectively at ourselves, to find the whole truth and nothing but the truth, even if it means recognizing that we have made mistakes and thus must make amends accordingly. What it also says is that you ought not to be judgmental about your actions or intentions or those of others.

You may find this card turning up when a decision is to be made, and, if it is in the "you now" position, you will be able to do so with a more rational viewpoint than you thought.

As a "past" card, it implies you have got what you deserve, you have accepted that the situation is now as it is because of what you said, did or didn't do in the past, and now things are set to improve. Whatever the results of a series of events, things will now begin to work out for you if you are truly honest and take responsibility for your choices.

Legal issues, settlements, debts paid, lawyers and other official systems are often signified by this card in a "future" position and will have a successful outcome. If you are seeking a new romance, drawing this card indicates that you'll get what you truly deserve, or a charming, diplomatic admirer will soon come into your life.

The Hanged Man

ARCANUM 12
ZODIAC AFFINITY Neptune

KEY WORDS

Transition, readjustment, limbo, paradox

KEY PHRASES

- *Sacrifice may be necessary*
- *Bored with life, anticipation of progress*
- *Static relationship*
- *Seeing life from a different angle*
- *Changing priorities*
- *Relinquishing control*
- *Take a step back to move forward*

Interpretation

One of the most mysterious cards in the tarot; the Hanged Man is paradoxical, mysterious and imbued with the frustration of trying to solve a cryptic crossword. The simplest interpretations are given first, followed by the more compelling but enriching paradox of this enigmatic card.

In a "you now" position, this card means you are at a crossroads and may have to stand back and look carefully at all the issues involved; or it may mean that you simply get out of a rut. You are in limbo about what you want to do next, or are going through a cease-fire in a relationship clash. The Hanged Man also warns you about whether to make sacrifices or not. Fine if you are ready to give up a bad influence in your life, but think clearly—have others really manipulated you or have you chosen to be a victim?

If chosen as a "future" card, you will undergo a change of mind, and will have to readjust your feelings in order to forge ahead with your plans.

The complexity of the Hanged Man invites you to do exactly the opposite of what you think is right to do, and thereby gain results. For example, you might be dying to call that fascinating stranger to go on a date, but are terrified they'll turn you down. If you draw the Hanged Man, it's more likely you'll go on that date if you don't make that phone call. The more you want something, the more you have to give up on the wanting and then it will happen. The paradox is that as soon as you make these contradictory moves, you find what you are actually seeking.

Finally, the Hanged Man says that it is time to let go of emotional baggage, and that you will soon be released from any pain or emotional hurt because you are opening your mind to living for the moment, not for the past.

Death

ARCANUM 13
ZODIAC AFFINITY Scorpio

KEY WORDS

Change, new beginnings, endings, transformation

KEY PHRASES

- *The end of an old cycle and the beginning of a new one*
- *Let go of the past, don't fear being true to yourself*
- *One door closes, another opens*
- *A parting of the ways*
- *Accepting the inevitable*
- *Getting down to the nitty-gritty*
- *Accepting the cycles of change*

Interpretation

This card often alarms people. But please don't take it literally. This is the one card in the pack upon which we project our greatest fears. But Death is a positive card in all positions, and remember, it is an archetypal energy, concerned with transition from one state to another. Something ends, something else begins, and gives you a chance to embrace change rather than fear it.

When Death appears in a spread, it simply implies that something has reached the end of a cycle. It could be a love affair, a job or a belief system that now needs to undergo some kind of transformation.

When in the "you now" position, Death can imply that you are in the process of changing your life but are perhaps concerned about the consequences. You might secretly want to end a love relationship but can't bear to hurt someone, or you need to change something about your life so that you can unleash your true potential.

In the "blockage" position, you fear change so much that you are stifled by that fear. Death here can also imply that changing circumstances are blocking your personal vision, and that you are confused about the next stage of your journey. Always relate this card directly to your question, issue or self-development mission, because then it will be more obvious what needs to change. As a "future" card, embrace the changes that are coming your way.

Temperance

ARCANUM 14
ZODIAC AFFINITY Sagittarius

KEY WORDS

Self-control, compromise, moderation, virtue

KEY PHRASES

- *The blending of ideas*
- *Harmony and understanding*
- *Moderation is the key to success*
- *Alchemical process*
- *Recognizing cooperation*
- *Healing energy*

Interpretation

Whenever you draw this card, good management of your relationship or personal world is in process. Although on the surface this card seems rather uninspiring or static, its underlying message is that through finding the middle way you will achieve your goals. There is harmony between your desires and your needs, and you are mentally and emotionally in balance.

This card often implies that if you moderate your indulgences, whether physical, emotional or spiritual, you will find equilibrium and balance.

If you are trying to make a decision, you will find a solution, and it will be much easier to see another person's point of view. As a "you now" card, your self-control and willingness to compromise are a good influence on others.

As a "blockage" card, it can mean that you are too willing to compromise. Trying to please everyone apart from yourself is at the root of your current issue or concern. Also it can indicate that someone you know is just being too good to be true, and they may not realize that you need their difference of opinion as well as their cooperation.

As a "future" card, you will have to moderate your desires and try to see both sides of an argument. But clarification of your true goals or aspirations is coming your way. There will soon be clarity, harmony and mutual respect, and healing energy for any existing emotional wounds or confusions will be generated by your search for the happy medium.

The Devil

ARCANUM 15
ZODIAC AFFINITY Capricorn

KEY WORDS
Bondage, materialism, living a lie, temptation

KEY PHRASES
- *Ignorance in relationship*
- *Thirst for money or power*
- *Unconscious reactions, childlike responses*
- *Self-imposed bondage*
- *Being obsessed*
- *Relinquishing control*
- *Chained to addictive patterns of behavior*
- *Manipulation by others*
- *Negative thinking*
- *Limited perception, generalization*

Interpretation

The Devil archetype is all that is apparently "bad" in a world where we constantly search for the good. The word "devil" derives from the Greek word *diablos*, which simply means "adversary." In fact, it is our own inner Devil who is usually the cause of most of our problems, generated by our lack of consciousness, by ignorance or illusions. The Devil appears when we are literally "in the dark."

The positive aspect of the Devil is that the card asks us to accept our limitations, to develop awareness of self and others, and to understand that we may be literally bound and chained to a narrow perspective or living under other people's expectations. How often do you hear "he's just like his father"; "women are all the same"; "I can't do that"; "power and money will make me happy." That is the real Devil in us speaking.

Generally in a layout, this card reveals that you are bound by your fears, beliefs or a situation that is unhealthy for you. You may be ignorant of the truth or blinded by illusion. Make sure you are not cheating on your values. When you draw this card it is timely to question your beliefs, viewpoint and goals. Whose are they anyway—yours or someone else's assumptions?

When this card is in the "you now" position, it can simply mean that you are attracted to someone for lust or money. Or you are getting involved in a relationship and are confusing sexual desire with love.

As a "blockage" card, the Devil suggests that you are living a lie about the current situation. As a "future" card, you are going to have to fight against the temptations of materialism, power, or self-deception. Take care that you are not led astray by someone who wants to take control over you or assert their power. Sometimes this card reveals that you are acting without awareness of your actions or the consequences of your actions.

The Tower

ARCANUM 16
ZODIAC AFFINITY Mars

KEY WORDS

External disruption, unexpected events, revelation

KEY PHRASES

- *Breakdown of the old to herald the new*
- *Acceptance that no defense is totally secure*
- *Learn to adapt and adjust quickly*
- *Suddenly seeing the truth of a matter*
- *Dramatic upheaval*
- *Having a change in fortune*
- *Unexpected challenges*
- *Chaos all around you*

Interpretation

There is or will be change in an unexpected and external manner when this card appears in a layout. This change appears as an outside catalyst and we feel we are not responsible for the disruption. But the disruption is usually liberating and it can free us from restriction and open us to fresh viewpoints. In a sense it is the catalyst needed to break free from the self-imposed chains of the previous card, the Devil.

Whatever happens can seem as if it is fated, that you are not responsible. But the Tower represents the structure you have built securely around yourself, your defense system, a crumbling old lighthouse warning danger. Sometimes locked within the many rooms of your lighthouse or tower are things that need throwing out, a declutter of emotions and feelings that no longer serve your current purpose.

The Tower's lightning strike is there to remind us that something needs to change. The inner world is just as unsafe as the outer and now is the time to be catapulted into awareness and be liberated from the old and worn out.

The Tower reveals that there is usually a catalyst or outside influence which comes into your life to instigate those changes. It can either be a person or a set of circumstances of which you feel you are not in control. It can be either liberating or uncomfortable, but you will now have the necessary strength to adapt and move on.

This card asks you to welcome new challenges rather than avoid them. Rebuild from renewed strength and reach a new level of understanding about your self and your situation.

In the "you now" position, it seems there is chaos all around you. As a "blockage" card, the Tower signifies your refusal to see the truth.

The Star

ARCANUM 17
ZODIAC AFFINITY Aquarius

KEY WORDS

Inspiration, ideal love, truth revealed

KEY PHRASES

- *Realization of a dream*
- *Insight and self-belief are essential for happiness*
- *Seeing the light at the end of the tunnel*
- *Knowing you are going to be successful*
- *Freely giving of yourself in love*
- *Idealization of a person or goal*
- *Visionary progress*
- *New trust in a relationship*

Interpretation

The Star represents all the heavenly bodies that guide us across land and seas. The ancients used the stars to navigate unknown waters and the archetype of the Star provides you with your own personal shining light that will allow you to navigate successfully through life.

When you draw this card, your powers of self-expression are at their highest. You feel in touch with universal energy and there is hope and belief in the future.

In the "you now" position, this card is all about having an optimistic attitude. If you really believe and trust in yourself you can create your own opportunities. This card is beneficial in any layout and indicates success in love, work or financial aspiration.

As a "future" card, it reveals that a revelation is about to come to you in the nicest possible way. You will regain your motivation, experience peace of mind and enjoy a better sense of who you are and where you are going.

The Star gives you permission to navigate wherever you want to go. But remember, this is a card of inspiration; it does not give practical solutions, so you must look to the other cards in the layout to guide you further. The only downside to this card is when it is in the "blockage" position, where it indicates that your ideals and expectations are so high that no one, not even you can live up to them.

The Moon

ARCANUM 18
ZODIAC AFFINITY Pisces

KEY WORDS

Intuition, fear, self-deceit, illusion

KEY PHRASES

- *Tricky love affair*
- *Blind to the truth, unrealistic dreams*
- *Feeling confused*
- *Feeling worried and apprehensive*
- *Trusting your intuition*
- *Losing touch with reality*

Interpretation

A complex card because its very nature is deceptive, the Moon is very concerned with our sense of belonging or safety and security. When you are in familiar surroundings or with people you know, you feel safe. But there are times when we experience the darker side of our own natures, the unknown shadowy bits trying to see the light of day. This can make us feel disoriented, afraid, vulnerable or anxious.

The Moon needs expression and when it occurs in a layout the positive aspect of the Moon is to trust in those deeper realms, and to remember that mystery permeates life at all times, although we usually refuse to acknowledge it. The illusion of the Moon is simply that; and the advice is not to let self-deception and distortion of the truth lead you astray or away from your purpose. You have a goal, so stick to it.

In the "you now" position, you may feel confused or unsure of what to do next. The Moon says to find your way, however hard it seems, or identify your fears. Trust in your instincts.

Interpret this card as a warning that things may not be all they seem. Maybe you are wrong, your judgment is unsound or someone is taking advantage of you. To fathom this one, try to tap into your intuition rather than your imagination because they are very different.

As a "blockage" card, the Moon suggests that your insecurities are holding you back, that you don't feel you belong to anything or anyone, maybe not even to yourself. As a "future" card, someone will be dishonest, either yourself or a partner or friend. The Moon also indicates that you are so wrapped up in your emotions and feelings that you don't have a clear rational view of the truth of a matter.

The Sun

ARCANUM 19
ZODIAC AFFINITY Sun

KEY WORDS

Communication, sharing, happiness, joy, positive energy, creativity, growth

KEY PHRASES

- *Accomplishment in love*
- *New friendship*
- *Feeling enlightened*
- *Positive accomplishment*
- *Believing in yourself*
- *Self-confidence*
- *Being the center of attention*
- *Shining under the spotlight*

The tarot directory

Interpretation

As a "you now" card, the Sun implies that it is time to communicate your feelings and express your dreams. This is a positive card and always signifies success and happiness. Where the Star gives us inspiration and direction, the Sun illuminates us with positive thoughts about how we can manifest those goals or dreams.

The Sun is the source of all life on this Earth; without it we wouldn't be here. The archetypal Sun represents courage, energy, insight and getting to the heart of a matter. With this card we can illuminate our lives with clarity and truth, rather than hide in the dark shadows of the Moon. The Sun encourages us to move on and leave those shadows behind. In reality your shadow will always be with you, but, as when standing in the midday sun, you hardly know it's there. You feel alive, brazen, prominent, regal.

If you have a relationship issue, in the "you now" position the Sun signifies that you can accept your friend or partner for who they are, rather than trying to change them (or vice versa).

As a "future" card, you can expect to be happier, fun-loving and liberated from past doubts and fears. Possibly a new fulfilling relationship will begin, not necessarily an intimate one, but one that will have a positive effect on your life. As a "blockage" card, you may be exaggerating how happy you are, only looking at the surface of a relationship or so concerned about personal glory that you aren't aware of the needs of others.

Judgement

ARCANUM 20
ZODIAC AFFINITY Pluto

KEY WORDS

Liberation, judgment, inner calling, transformation

KEY PHRASES

- *Accounting for past actions*
- *Revaluation and revival*
- *Dropping old values, embracing new ones*
- *Accepting things the way they are*
- *There is no one to blame, not even yourself*

Interpretation

There are two types of judgment: one where we judge others unkindly or unfairly by saying things like "You are no good" or "I disapprove of your actions"; and the other kind, which does not condemn, but attempts to weigh up the matter and to find out the truth. When we draw Judgement in a layout it signifies the latter—that we must make choices and do so without blaming ourselves or others.

Judgment implies that you can liberate yourself from old attitudes, whether toward a lover, your family or patterns of behavior that haven't been right for you. You have new insight into how to handle your relationships. It is fine to shrug your shoulders and think "what's the point?" but this is your chance to start afresh, let go of the past and stop feeling guilty for your actions.

As a "blockage" card, you are likely to feel guilty in some way for something or feel judged by others. Perhaps it's timely to think about whether you are in the wrong or whether you are taking too much responsibility for someone else's happiness?

As a "future" card you will have to make decisions by facing up to the facts rather than avoiding them. With Judgement you can at last get off the fence, make choices and wake up to new possibilities. There is a feeling of a weight being taken off your shoulders and the ability to forgive yourself or someone else for past mistakes.

The World

ARCANUM 21
ZODIAC AFFINITY Saturn

KEY WORDS

Completion, fulfillment, freedom, cosmic love, freedom from fear

KEY PHRASES

- *Reward for hard work and effort*
- *Time for celebration of self and others*
- *Feeling the world is your oyster*
- *Traveling both physically and mentally*
- *Accomplishing what you set out to achieve*
- *Discovering a solution*
- *Feeling at one with yourself and the universe*

Interpretation

The World is always a positive card in any layout. It signifies that you are becoming more aware of who you are, your limitations, your choices and taking responsibility for yourself.

In the "you now" position, it means you are coming to terms with yourself, your sense of individual value and how you relate to others. The World can also mean you've met the ultimate partner, found the perfect vocation, and there is no turning back. Whatever the cost involved, you know that you have to move forward, turn down another pathway and follow the signpost.

As a "blockage" card, you could be too convinced that everything is going well or you are simply indulging in too much wishful thinking. You may need to ask yourself questions such as "What is my true potential? Who am I? What do I need to wake up to?" You may be seeing only what you want to see or living by others' expectations of how you should behave. Perhaps it's time to take a more objective look at yourself and your goals.

As a "future" card, you can look forward to success in relationships and all creative enterprises. Sometimes this card is interpreted as "the world is yours." You might be about to embark on a trip of a lifetime, whether literally around the world or into a new venture. In all kinds of ways you are expanding your horizons, both emotionally and physically, and you know that if you follow the right path your future happiness will be assured.

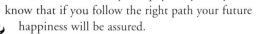

The
Minor
Arcana

Understanding the Minor Arcana

The Minor Arcana consist of 56 cards made up of four suits—Swords, Wands, Pentacles and Cups. Each suit has 14 cards: numbers Ace (1) through to 10, and four court cards—Page, Knight, Queen and King.

Remember these associations from the introduction:

The court cards

Each court card is a personification of the symbol of that suit, in other words, personality types or characters that tell you more about your life journey from the outside looking in. They can represent people you meet in everyday life who are signposts on your journey. They may be people you already know and the different facets of your own personality that you project onto others.

The rank of the court card will also tell you the type of energy that is being expressed, either by yourself or a person who is important in your life.

Kings

Always dynamic, Kings represent power and charisma. They reveal that action or extrovert energy must be expressed or that someone you know or meet in your daily life will be a dynamic force for changes or choices to be made. Kings also represent maturity or male authority figures.

Queens

Passive, yet creative, Queens represent the power of the feminine, the qualities of understanding, protection, nurture and receptivity, whether in a man or in a woman. Queens also represent caring mothers, women who want to be on a throne or a female authority figure you know.

Knights

Pushy and extreme, Knights express the suit quality at its best and worst. These cards have a kind of immature adult feel about them. They reflect the extremes of energy of the suit. For example, the Knight of Pentacles suggests someone who will be shrewd about money, but also unlikely ever to take a financial risk for fear of "doing the wrong thing." Knights can also represent immature friends, family or lovers, men under 30 or those who are free from responsibility.

Pages

The energy represented by the Pages is lighthearted, childish and fickle. Pages can also refer to very young teenagers, children or a very immature adult. They also represent a playful spirit, the opportunist, the need to grab something that is offered.

Court card exercise

Before looking at each individual interpretation for the court cards, try this simple exercise.

1 Make a list of people you know who might be represented by the Queens, Kings, Pages and Knights.

2 List the "positive" attributes and the "negatives" of the court cards. Knights, for example, are obvious. They represent extremes of behavior. Queens, however, seem to be all goodness and light. Think about any Queen-like people you know. Are they actually wielding power by being kind and gentle? Are they truly on the "throne" because they want to be there or is it because they want to be the center of everyone's else's world?

3 Now direct the same ideas to yourself. What are your King, Queen, Page and Knight energies? How well developed is the King in you? Are you too dominant or too passive? Are you a Knight who rushes in where angels fear to tread or the kind of Knight who makes a point by being stubborn and rigorous (Pentacles)? Are you in touch with your inner Page? In what state is your child within? Playful, adventurous and cheeky, or lost in the world of convention and adult responsibility?

The number cards

These cards represent events, areas of life in which you will meet, discover and experience yourself, and the arenas, places and themes where you will find out more about who you are. They include affairs, activities and concerns that we encounter on a day-to-day basis.

The Universal tarot pack used in this book has very clear illustrations on each numbered card, so it is quite easy to interpret the card simply from the images alone. However, many packs such as the Marseille pack and the ancient Minchiate deck use only the number and pip symbols.

Each number has a strong affinity with both numerology and astrology (see pages 352–363), but below is a quick checklist of meanings for each of the numbered suit cards.

Key words to the number cards

NUMBER	KEY WORDS
Ace	Beginnings, vitality, new opportunities
Two	Balancing events, duality, doubling strength or splitting power
Three	Creativity, results, achievement
Four	Limitations, doubts, holding back
Five	Versatility, communication, opening up
Six	Harmony, idealism, inner peace
Seven	Dreams, illusions, magic
Eight	Overcoming obstacles, easing restrictions
Nine	Action, courage, self-confidence
Ten	Endings and beginnings, new destinations, fulfillment

Suit of Wands

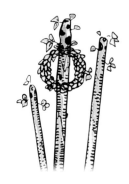

Wands (also known as Staffs, Clubs, Sceptres, Rods and Batons) are traditionally linked to the element of fire. They are often represented as fiery brands, long staves or rods, or branches of trees with new shoots sprouting from the bark as in the Universal tarot. This represents a sign of new growth, literally the spark of life.

This suit is about creativity, passion, enterprise and initiative. When you draw a majority of Wands in a layout, this indicates that you are ready for action, up for adventure, that you are impatient or just so impetuous that you don't have time to sit and think things through properly. Impulsive action, invention and clear perception are also fiery qualities. And, like the fire signs Aries, Leo and Sagittarius, Wands signify vision, intention and a future-oriented outlook on life. However, a predominance of Wands in a spread can also signify you are taking on more than you can handle.

KEY WORDS
Positive qualities:
Drive, self-motivation, will, vision, energy, desire, competition, boldness, defiance, charm
Negative qualities:
Restlessness, empty promises, egotism, pride, foolhardiness, hot-temperedness

Suit of Wands exercise

Before looking up each interpretation for the suit of Wands, try this exercise to help you get to know the cards.

1 Lay the Wand court cards face up toward you in ascending order—Page, Knight, Queen, King.

2 Think about people you know who are fiery, spirited individuals and who might identify with each of the characters.

3 Next, think about yourself. Are you fiery? Do you associate easily with this quality? Does it make you angry, happy, indifferent or peaceful? Think about your reaction to this energy and whether you are enjoying it, denying it or repressing its presence in your own psyche.

4 Look at the different images of the numbered cards. You don't have to remember what each number means to understand the meaning of these very vivid cards. Most of the numbered cards are people seeking, doing, acting in some particular way. These are *energizing* cards, so always interpret them as action rather than inaction.

Ace of Wands

KEY WORDS

New beginnings, originality, creative vision, fresh start, adventure

KEY PHRASES

- *Have belief in your abilities*
- *Know the right way forward*
- *Face up to the facts*
- *Sexual initiative is now required*
- *Act on inspirational ideas*
- *Come up with a solution to a problem*
- *Feelings of excitement*
- *Be passionate about life*

Interpretation

Like all aces, the Ace of Wands suggests initiating a new venture or a sense of wonder and newness about beginning something afresh. But, because Wands are about energy and action, this card signifies doing something out there in the external world to get results. It is not just about thinking inspirational thoughts, but acting upon them too.

In a "you now" position, the Ace of Wands suggests that the spirit of enterprise is now yours to play with. Whether it is a creative idea that has been lurking at the back of your mind, or a sudden gush of optimism and courage, it is time to act on that feeling of enthusiasm.

Alternatively, in a "future" position, it indicates that great opportunities or exciting events are available. It is up to you to push for what you want, to take the lead and show you mean business. This card also suggests originality and creativity, and that it is time to trust your instincts and follow through.

In a relationship issue, this card says "get on with it," enjoy a more lively direction, be creative with your love life rather than let it stagnate.

In the "blockage" position, the Ace of Wands indicates that you are being too pushy or self-assured and your individual desires are stopping you from making headway with others. You may be up for taking on the world, but you must also look carefully at your limitations.

Two of Wands

KEY WORDS

Achievement, courage, worldly desires, personal power

KEY PHRASES

- *Feeling you have the whole world in your hands*
- *Persuading others of your talents*
- *Having the courage to prove your point*
- *Making your mark on the world*
- *Showing you mean business*
- *Being inventive and different*
- *Embracing new ideas*
- *Widening your perspective*
- *Feeling that you are omnipotent*

Interpretation

Two is the number of doubling strength or splitting power. The Two of Wands emphasizes our need to assert ourselves, and to find our own level of personal power. When this card appears in the "you now" position, you will feel as if you have been given carte blanche to wield your power or that you have been filled with the ambrosia of the gods. In some ways it is like drinking a few glasses of champagne and believing yourself capable of saying and doing all those things you were fearful of before.

The Two of Wands makes you feel as if you are in touch with a Divine power, which of course can lead to hubris and arrogance. Be careful if you get this card in the "blockage" position; however invigorated or empowered you feel right now, don't let that sense of omnipotence blind you to your true needs and intentions. The Two of Wands can also indicate that someone else is trying to exert power over you if you choose this card in a relationship spread.

As a "future outcome" card, the time is right for initiative and invention. It is time to take the bull by the proverbial horns and show you are a force to be reckoned with. Again, remember the power is working through you, and Two means that sometimes, rather than merely doubling up your sense of power, you might have to share the power with someone else to make a success of your plans. Perhaps you should become the power behind the throne, rather than just on it?

Three of Wands

KEY WORDS

Foresight, expansion, exploration, contemplation

KEY PHRASES

- *Seeking new adventure*
- *Following up new clues*
- *Seeing how best to act*
- *Knowing what is going to happen next*
- *Having an open perspective*
- *Starting on a new journey*
- *Awareness of your intentions*
- *Knowledge as power*
- *A sense of vocation*

Interpretation

A highly creative card, the Three of Wands indicates that it is time to explore future possibilities with foresight and a sense of adventure. Rather like the figure on the card, you are standing on the hilltop looking across the terrain ahead of you. Aware of the threshold, you have a chance to look ahead before you take a new path.

It is timely to reflect on what you know to be right for you and what is available. This is not a card about taking a risk; rather, like any real explorer, you set off with provisions, a map, plans and knowledge of the territory. Is it going to be a barren landscape or is there something calling you on?

When you draw this card in a "you now" position, it is time to work with your plans, unleash your knowledge and start to show others you know the way forward. Rather like Prometheus in Greek mythology (whose name, incidentally, means "foresight"), you are about to embark on a great adventure, but remember to give back something to the world rather than do it solely for personal profit. Prometheus stole fire from the gods to give to mankind and was accordingly punished by being chained to a rock every day.

This is not your future, simply that you must be prepared to pay the price for your quest by anticipating the obstacles on the way. You are asked to move courageously onward but with foresight as your greatest gift right now. However, if you choose this card in the "blockage" position, you are too obsessed with what will happen next to see the truth of where you are now.

Four of Wands

KEY WORDS

Celebration, joy, spontaneity, freedom

KEY PHRASES

- *Exuberant about life or love*
- *Enjoying a happy event*
- *Domestic harmony*
- *Mutual celebration*
- *Feeling proud of your achievements*
- *Being released from the chains of responsibility*
- *Feeling freer than a bird*
- *Dumping emotional baggage*
- *Freeing yourself from others' expectations*

Interpretation

Congratulations! This card is a blessing to have in any layout as it heralds a time for rejoicing and celebrating. It can also imply dancing toward harmony and that happier times are ahead. When in the "you now" position, you have fresh confidence about your intentions and are finally at a point when you can feel proud of anything you've accomplished.

There is also a sense of lively anticipation when you draw the Four of Wands. The inner child in you is being nudged to come out from hiding under that adult guise and indulge in fun. Laugh a little, get involved in more social interaction, spread your lighthearted charisma around. In a "blockage" position, you may be overdoing the merrymaking at the expense of something more important or denying the serious aspects of life for all the more laid-back possibilities. Because you fear moving on, making changes or looking at the truth of who you really are, you compensate through sheer self-congratulation and nonstop socializing.

In a "future" position, the Four of Wands can represents events and people who will come into your world to lighten up your life. Excitement is about to be generated, and planned parties or celebrations are well-favored.

The Four of Wands also indicates that you can now free yourself from any circumstances that don't suit you. Whether it is a relationship, job, self-doubt or fear, you can break free and open yourself to new possibilities or cut loose from self-imposed bonds. It is time to move into the next phase of personal growth and leave the past behind.

Five of Wands

KEY WORDS
Competition, rivalry, minor setbacks, disagreement

KEY PHRASES
- *Quarreling over nothing*
- *Feeling you don't know where you stand*
- *Indulging in competition*
- *Feeling challenged or persecuted*
- *Trying to defend yourself unsuccessfully*
- *Frustrating circumstances*
- *Hassled by other people's opinions*
- *Irritating hiccups*

Interpretation

The Five of Wands conveys that there is a struggle of some kind, yet it is hard to know who is going to come out the winner. Similarly, when you draw the Five of Wands you may feel as if you have to pick a fight, perhaps mentally within yourself, or else challenge someone out in the external world.

In the "you now" position, this card indicates that you feel as if the world is against you right now. That everything you do is unwelcome or goes wrong. You call a friend, she's gone on holiday without her cell phone. The toothpaste is stuck, the toast lands butter side down, the key doesn't fit the lock. It is those irritating minor hiccups in life that this card represents, but it can feel like a mighty challenge. It feels as if someone or something is working at cross-purposes against you.

This card can also imply that you are at odds with yourself, too; that what you think you want or need isn't in accordance with what you truly need or want. It is time to stop battling with yourself and set down your true priorities.

On another level, this card stands for pure competition. You do have rivals out there, so what is the point in denying it? Maybe they are after the same job, lover or simply for the first place in the lineup. The clue to working with this card is to start to cooperate. Begin to find an agreement between you and others or you and yourself, and learn to work toward finding harmony in your life.

As a "blockage" card, the Five of Wands indicates that you are trying too hard to rise above the competition, which inevitably means you will end up at the bottom of the heap, or you feel so persecuted by others that your scapegoat tactics are stopping you from involving yourself in a real relationship.

Six of Wands

KEY WORDS

Pride, victory, reward, accomplishment

KEY PHRASES

- *Receiving acclaim for your actions*
- *Being the center of attention*
- *Feeling accomplished*
- *Looking after number one*
- *Taking it all in your stride*
- *Getting on your high horse*
- *Being too proud to admit the truth*
- *Feeling superior*

Interpretation

The Six of Wands represents triumph at its most pure and untainted. The problem is that when we feel we've won, come out on top or simply are the best at something, we can get carried away on a wave of self-aggrandisement. So when you see this card in the "you now" position, do take care that you're not so involved in yourself that you refuse to come down off your high horse.

Humility is needed when this card is drawn, but that doesn't mean you can't pat yourself on the back. There are times when we all need to feel we're victorious, but with that kind of recognition don't forget the feelings of others in the excitement. If you draw this as a "blockage" card, then self-inflation is preventing you from following your true path.

As a "future" card, success or rewards are coming your way, or someone who is talented could come into your world to change it for the better. Remember that "pride comes before a fall," too. If you don't trip over your own gold-pointed shoes, then fine, look forward to the triumph, but never forget that disaster could be part of the deal, too. The latter comes from believing that you are the only one with the right to be successful.

Alternatively, as a "future outcome" card, you will soon find great value in looking after number one or proving that you have a right to gain, to triumph or acclaim which is due to you. "If you can meet with triumph and disaster and treat those two impostors just the same" is a phrase that sums up this card.

Seven of Wands

KEY WORDS

Defiance, purpose, gaining advantage

KEY PHRASES

- *Refusing to budge on principle*
- *Sticking to your guns*
- *Going for broke*
- *Defending yourself*
- *Confidence to say "no"*
- *Being resolute*
- *Strength against adversaries*
- *Fighting a pointless battle*
- *Aggressive interaction*
- *Struggling with the opposition*

Interpretation

When you draw the Seven of Wands, defiance and self-belief are strongly indicated. You may now be in a position to stand your ground and assert your needs or rights. This is not a passive card, but one where you must face criticism or defend yourself against some kind of opposition.

In the "you now" position, the time is right to say "no" rather than to compromise for the sake of argument. The image of the Seven of Wands is of a warrior meeting resistance from unknown sources. And it is often those unknown sources within ourselves, our own inner demons, that stop us from actually following our true beliefs and convictions. These inner demons are unconscious patterns of behavior that rise up within us when we feel threatened by change or crucial decision-making. They are simply our deeper fears and doubts that take over and make us weak and vulnerable.

The Seven of Wands suggests resisting those fears, being honest about what you personally want and taking action accordingly.

In the "blockage" position, this card indicates that you are having a battle with your conscience, or that you find it difficult to make a stand or resist others' beliefs and demands.

In the "future" position, you will soon have to invest time and energy in confronting any opposition to your plans. But, like any defense, you must also decide if something is worth fighting for. How important is your choice or decision? Does it serve your true values or someone else's, and do you have just cause for your actions? This card reminds you to have the courage of your convictions, but make sure you know what they are.

Eight of Wands

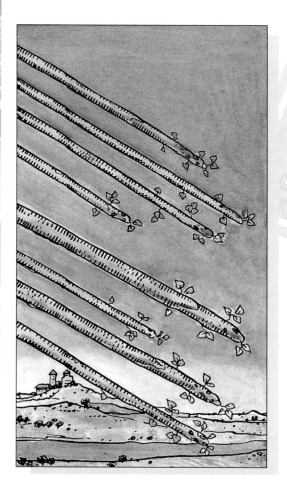

KEY WORDS
Rushing ahead, action, news, options

KEY PHRASES
- *Getting your priorities sorted out*
- *Making clear your intentions*
- *Taking swift action*
- *Receiving an important message*
- *Discovering the missing link*
- *Quick developments*
- *Reevaluating decisions*
- *Everything is up in the air*
- *Taking stock of the situation*

Interpretation

The Eight of Wands portrays a set of wands or staves moving through the air. This card embodies a feeling of movement, but the feeling is neither grounded nor finalized. It is ongoing, fast and furious, ideological and speculative rather than real and solid. The Eight of Wands represents those ideas and actions within yourself that are intuitive, generated by sudden flashes, thoughts or reactions to events, and are not static.

The card signifies that it is time either to get your priorities sorted out because things are so up in the air, or to make it clear what your intentions are right now.

It also indicates that you are simply rushing ahead with your plans, or that taking swift action is essential. What you learn from this card is that if you act now and don't hesitate, things will work out as you wish.

As a "blockage" card, the Eight of Wands signifies that you are in flight, you are unsure of what your next course of action is, and constantly shifting the goal posts won't result in a goal. You need to come down to earth and ground those ideas.

In a "future" or "outcome" position, be prepared for news and fresh information which you might not recognize due to its method of delivery. Keep your eyes and your mind open for any possibility that can lead you to the truth of a particular issue. There may be so many ideas floating around at the same time that you will feel overwhelmed by the choices, but regard them as resources to help you make a decision.

Nine of Wands

KEY WORDS

Preparedness, at the ready, defensiveness, strength, awareness

KEY PHRASES

- *Feeling vulnerable and cautious*
- *Defending yourself "just in case"*
- *Remembering past hurts*
- *Feeling worried about the future*
- *Developing strength through self-awareness*
- *Prepared for anything*
- *Persistence and perseverance*
- *Suspicion of others*

Interpretation

Whatever you have been through, whether emotional pain or a bad relationship experience, this card indicates that you are now prepared to move on. In developing your strength you have gained wisdom and self-awareness, but you are still cautious about encountering the same experiences. In life we carry many wounds; we all go through bad times. Like the figure on the Nine of Wands, it is not so much about regretting the past, feeling resentful or licking your wounds with a vengeful eye; it is more about knowing that we make mistakes, have failures and learn from life's lessons.

Be watchful, be wary of your vulnerability, but don't become acutely defensive or bitter, or you could lose out. The Nine of Wands indicates an ability to "see" your strengths and weaknesses; to acknowledge your pitfalls and potentials; to stay alert to those facts and to persevere at all costs, whatever the challenge.

In a "blockage" position, you may be so defensive that no one can get close to you or a current relationship is suffering because you are still hanging on to emotional baggage. In the "future" position, refuse to take "no" for an answer, persist, be resourceful, and most of all "know thyself" as the oracle has written above the Temple of Apollo.

Ten of Wands

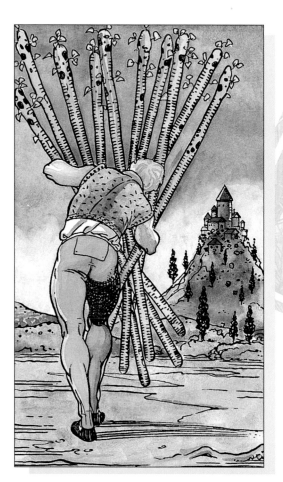

KEY WORDS

Heavy burden, overload, uphill struggle

KEY PHRASES

- *Taking on too much responsibility*
- *Being too willing to please*
- *Overextending yourself*
- *All work and no play*
- *Feeling you are to blame for everything*
- *Believing there is always a price to pay*
- *Resigned to being a workhorse*
- *Feeling accountable*
- *Struggling with your workload*
- *Blocked thinking*

Interpretation

Whenever this card appears in a layout, it indicates that you have some kind of burden which you are carrying. Before you immediately put your finger on the cause—too much work, too much duty, too much anything—think about whether your perception of life is in need of a revamp. Is it possible that you are so wrapped up in the normal "burdens" of life that you have no direction, no current goal or just can't see where you're going?

This card signifies that it is time to lighten the load. To drop some of your tasks, delegate, cut back and take time out for pleasure and play. We often "hang on" to people in our relationships. We work hard to make a relationship work for fear of rejection; we try to please too much as a way of keeping control of the relationship. This card asks you to expand your awareness, and to see the value of other viewpoints or that letting go of the huge burden you've created for yourself won't mean you give up on yourself.

Perhaps you need to take more time to devote to you and your personal journey. And a partner, lover or relative won't stop loving you because you devote a little more time to pleasing yourself rather than them.

In the "future" position, you might have to go through a bit of an uphill struggle, so lighten the load, let others help you rather than nobly thinking you can do everything yourself. You may blame yourself for the events that unfold, but remember there is no one to blame in life. The Ten of Wands says stop feeling guilty, responsible or overcommitted and give more time to the lighter aspects of life. Aren't they just as valuable?

The deepest level of interpretation of this card is that our very burdens are what force us to carry on and win at all costs.

Page of Wands

KEY WORDS

A messenger, new insight, fresh ideas, confidence

KEY PHRASES

- *Willing to go in a new direction*
- *Showing you have enthusiasm*
- *Being creative*
- *A charming admirer*
- *Taking a chance*
- *Childlike exuberance*
- *Lighthearted energy*

Interpretation

When you draw the Page of Wands, you are receiving a message that it is time to start afresh, to look at all the options and be inspired by what you see before you. You have chances for new opportunities in love, perhaps a younger admirer, seductive charmers or simply lighthearted fun and romantic games.

If you are concentrating on a relationship issue, you have new insight into how to keep a relationship alive and exciting. You may, however, be distracted from current projects because someone new or a tantalizing offer comes into your life at this time. In the "blockage" position, you may be so entranced by original ideas or people that you are tempted to drop everyone that you believed in before. Make sure that you complete all projects you have started when you see this card, otherwise there could be many loose ends to tie up when this energy has passed.

Sometimes the Page of Wands in the "you now" position implies that you are so full of childlike exuberance that there is no way right now you could commit yourself to any long-term plans. As a "future" outcome card, you are about to enter a phase of fresh optimism and passionate fun. Just go out there and enjoy yourself; the more confident and inspired you are, the more success you will have.

The Page of Wands is always the first to put up his hand, to show willing, to leap in at the deep end but, unlike the Fool who really doesn't care what is around the next corner and is blind to the outcome of his choices, the Page of Wands has enough self-belief and confidence to focus on what will be successful for him in the long term.

Remember, all the court cards represent facets of your own personality that you might project onto others. So, if a lighthearted "Peter Pan" figure comes into your life, they are there to remind you that you have a mischievous charming side that needs expression, too.

Knight of Wands

KEY WORDS

Impetuous, daring, impatient, passionate

KEY PHRASES

- *Gift of the gab but bragging*
- *Self-assured but vain*
- *Charming but insensitive*
- *Seductive but lustful*
- *Enthusiastic but makes empty promises*
- *Accomplished but exaggerates truth*
- *Loves to be loved but hates to be possessed*
- *Likes to depart but not to arrive*
- *Adventurous and daring but restless and unreliable*

Interpretation

As you can see from the key words and key phrases, the Knight of Wands represents extremes of energy. These traits can be seen as either positive or negative depending on your situation. For example, we tend to admire someone who is accomplished, but despise someone who exaggerates the truth or tells little white lies. Yet sometimes the truth needs to be exaggerated or a little white lie told to help a process unfold, or to serve the needs of the other without hurting them. It is all about our personal perception of the quality surrounding the word and how we experience it ourselves.

Remember that when you draw the Knight of Wands, this is all about vivacity, adventure and action. If in the "you now" position, it is time to be a little reckless, be passionate about life, don't fear your restlessness, do something with it. Express your daring streak and try something different.

It might also refer to a "knight in shining armor" who comes dashing into your life without a thought for who you are, but who is just there to show off, brag or seduce you. There is often a strong physical attraction to the opposite sex when you draw this card in the "current" or "future" positions.

In the "blockage" position, the card can mean that either you are totally infatuated with a heartbreaker, someone who won't be tied down, or you are involved in a sexual relationship that may fizzle out as fast as it began. Equally, your own hot-blooded desire for sexual or romantic conquest is dealing out the wrong kind of lovers.

In any issue or question that doesn't refer to relationships, you aren't thinking things through, you are too impulsive or insensitive to the heart of the matter. As a "future outcome" card, be prepared for some excitement in the future—travel, adventures or footloose and fancy-free individuals come charging into your life. Make way for both extremes of energy that the Knight of Wands represents and simply enjoy.

Queen of Wands

KEY WORDS

Magnetic, attractive, feminine leader, sexual fertility, optimistic, self-assured and upbeat

KEY PHRASES

- *Dedicated to a task*
- *Friendly and easygoing*
- *Wholeheartedly involved*
- *Charismatic and creative*
- *Woman who knows where she is going*
- *Sexually accomplished*
- *Undaunted by a challenge*
- *Brightens up the atmosphere*
- *Never fazed*

Interpretation

The Queen of Wands knows what she wants and where she is going. The black cat at her feet indicates that she is in touch with all aspects of the feminine and can express herself freely and confidently without worrying about what people think of her.

When you draw this card, fiery, charismatic individuals are indicated, particularly Leo-born women. In the "you now" position, you are going through a phase of upbeat, magnetic energy that needs expression. Don't deny yourself the right to be as accomplished and attractive as you want. Treat yourself to a new hairstyle, change your wardrobe, maximize your chances of financial or business success. Be aware of your direction and use your intuition to follow through.

In the current position, you are also dedicated to a cause, optimistic and enthusiastic for any new change or development in your life. Ask yourself right now if you are as confident as you can be; do you think you are attractive, and if not, why not do something about it? You radiate an aura of vibrancy and spirit, so get out there and enjoy your current well-being.

As a "blockage" card, there may be a woman in your social or business circle who is preventing you from discovering your own popularity. Alternatively, you are so self-assured and dedicated that you may have forgotten that you have a vulnerable side.

As a "future" card, you will soon be able to make a powerful impression where it counts. Sometimes the Queen represents a man or a woman who comes into your life exuding sex appeal and reminding you of your own sexual accomplishments.

King of Wands

KEY WORDS
Powerful, bold, inspiring, vitality, dramatic

KEY PHRASES
- *Mastering an art*
- *Setting an example*
- *A powerful leader*
- *Inspirational authority figure*
- *Theatrical and charismatic*
- *Role model*
- *Willing to take a risk based on insight*
- *Likes to be center-stage*
- *Never modest or shy*
- *Boldly confident*

Interpretation

When you draw the King of Wands, the energy is vibrant and vital, and there is a sense of drama and action in whatever you do. This fiery king is often literally represented by male authority figures with charisma and talent.

As a "you now" card, it signifies that you have learned from your mistakes, taken stock of your limitations and gained new abilities. You are now able to draw on this insight to move forward into the future without arrogance or vanity. You can view yourself from a larger perspective, although not totally objectively since you have a larger-than-life attitude to the world and everyone in it. Now is the time to take a few risks based on insight, knowledge and self-belief.

The inspirational energy of the King of Wands says "go out and do your thing," be bold and intrepid and put on a showcase performance, now is your chance. In the "blockage" position, the King of Wands signifies that someone in power is holding you back or that you have issues around power that need to be addressed before you can achieve your current goals. As a "future" card, the King indicates that soon you will be able to mastermind your projects or goals, that your power of individuality will get results or that your innovative ideas will get you places.

Suit of Cups

Cups (also known as Chalices) represent human feeling and emotion and the power of love or lack of it. The Cups tell us how we relate to each other and the external world beyond our own little world. We perceive this world through a lens colored by our own personality, psyche or experiences, and the Cups remind us about the way we relate to the external as well as inner world on a daily basis. The positive benefit of this suit is to give you clear indications of love, romance, sensuality, creative expression and the choices or issues that can arise from these areas in your life.

KEY WORDS

Human emotion, love, friendship, sensual pleasure, connection, intuition

Suit of Cups exercise

Before looking up each interpretation for the suit of Cups, try this exercise to help you get to know the cards.

1 Lay the court cards face up toward you in ascending order —Page, Knight, Queen, King—as you did for the suit of Wands.

2 Think about people you know who are watery, sensitive individuals and whom you might identify with each of the characters.

3 Next think about yourself. Are you emotional? Do you associate easily with your feelings? Does it make you angry, happy, indifferent, peaceful, or simply turn cold when you talk about feelings? Think about your reaction to this energy and whether you are enjoying it, denying it or repressing its validity in your own psyche.

4 Look at the different images on the numbered cards. You don't have to remember what each number means to understand the meaning of these very vivid cards. Most of the numbered cards are people *relating* to the world, they are engaging in their feelings and reactions to what is going on around them. Always think of these as relationship cards.

Ace of Cups

KEY WORDS

Love, deep feeling, new romance, intimacy

KEY PHRASES

- *Beginning of new love or awareness*
- *Expressing your feelings*
- *Being in touch with your emotions*
- *Infatuation with someone or something*
- *Establishing new bonds*
- *Feelings developing*
- *Desire for a deeper connection*

Interpretation

When you draw the Ace of Cups, the early stages of love or romance are indicated. You may find your feelings have intensified, or that you are falling head over heels in love with someone or something. We can just as easily become infatuated by an idea as we are by a lover. If you are already attached, there may be a stronger bond developing between you, or emotional needs to be expressed.

If you draw this card, look at the aspects of your life where love might be lacking or working for you. Are you really in touch with your own feelings, is it time to open up, sympathize with others, get closer to a friend, lover or family member? Are you giving too freely?

If this card falls in a "blockage" position, you are letting your emotions take over from the reality of a situation. As a "you now" card, the Ace of Cups also suggests that it is time to get in touch with the more spiritual aspects of your relationship. There is a strong mystical affinity in the images on the card, reminding us to let creative Divine energy into our lives, rather than simply attending to our ego desires. Look at the card and see what is offered, because this card can also indicate that a gift, encounter or opportunity is there for you to take, but you must be open to possibilities.

In a "future outcome" position, you merely have to open your eyes to see the truth and recognize what could be yours. Whether to gain access to deeper intimacy, to explore your own consciousness or to develop your spiritual direction, never reject what the Ace of Cups has to offer. Another gift that may be waiting in the wings is an enriched sexual affinity with someone, or that you must trust in your intuition and deeper feelings to guide you to make a choice.

Two of Cups

KEY WORDS

Relationship, connection, partnership, attraction

KEYWORDS

- *Moving toward another*
- *Alchemical merger*
- *Sexual attraction*
- *Romantic love*
- *Establishing a bond*
- *Mutual understanding*
- *Harmony and cooperation*
- *Reconciliation and forgiveness*

Interpretation

The Two of Cups is very like the Lovers in the Major Arcana, although it does not carry such profound archetypal symbolism. When you draw the Two of Cups, relationships are boldly highlighted. Look at the image: two lovers are facing each other, offering their cups, sharing their feelings, approaching one another to form a bond.

If you are looking for love or have just met someone, this is just the card you want to draw as a "future" card to generate that magnetic attraction. If you are already in a love relationship, then this card also suggests you are now in a state of harmony, or will be if drawn as an "outcome" card. But, to achieve that harmony, you must both learn to respect and accept your separateness. Neither should try to impose their expectations on the other.

The Two of Cups can suggest a marriage, or marriage of minds, or the alchemical energy of merging and blending to turn lead into gold. But you can only do so if you do not try to have power over the other.

With this card in the "you now" position, it is timely to join forces with someone to mutually experience nurturing and healing. If in the "blockage" position, this card can indicate that you are so wrapped up in your "twosome" that you are not able to stand alone or be creative with your own individual needs or values. It also signifies that your exclusive arrangement is stopping you from developing as two individuals. This twinning energy is very powerful, but it can mean that you lose touch with other kinds of love, because you are sending out signals of "don't come near" to all around.

But this card is mainly beneficial, and as a "future" card you can anticipate great mutual attraction with someone, or a sense of the union of opposites, both sexually and emotionally. Just take care that you aren't simply in love with love or the idea of neverending romance.

Three of Cups

KEY WORDS

Friendship, celebration, team spirit, exuberance

KEY PHRASES

- *Abundance and healing*
- *Enjoying your social network*
- *Making friends*
- *Being part of a group*
- *Sharing your happy feelings*
- *Community spirit*
- *Putting trust in others*
- *Celebratory rituals*

Interpretation

After Two, comes Three. We now have to share our feelings with more than one other. This card represents the ability to widen our feelings, to give out our joy and happiness to more than one person, and to start to interact with small groups of people who will boost our own sense of happiness and spirit.

This card is all about the spirit of the community or joining in the dance. Whether you need to make new friends or become a fully paid-up member of the team, this card says celebrate your inclusion in human compassion, empathy and consolidation.

We all need friends and, if you draw this card in the "you now" position, it indicates that through networking and social contact you will find an increased sense of security or happiness.

In a relationship issue, the Three of Cups also signifies that it is time to rejoice in your personal growth, to make new plans and create a way to share your abundance and sense of harmony. Be more laid-back, enjoy the company of friends or simply dance your way through the night. Celebrations don't have to be after the event; they can also be a way to generate creativity and fresh ideas when joining in with the spirit of the group.

This card also represents all forms of support from groups and social contacts. Check out your relationships with groups of people. Do you feel comfortable with just one person, insecure with three or four, vulnerable in a crowd? Or do you like to stand out from the crowd, organize events and watch from the wings, or mingle with the party throng? This card asks you to discover how you "relate" to a group, and how connected you feel to people on a collective level.

As a "blockage" card, you might be spending so much time partying or indulging in social niceties that you haven't given yourself enough individual time alone to sort out your priorities.

Four of Cups

KEY WORDS

Doubt, hesitation, introspection

KEY PHRASES

- *Lack of relationship to oneself*
- *Taking things personally*
- *Withdrawal and self-doubt*
- *Only concerned with yourself*
- *Contemplation for healing purposes*
- *Self-questioning*
- *Giving little away*
- *Not seeing what is available*
- *Feeling hurt and defensive*
- *Lacking initiative*
- *Apathetic and passive*

Interpretation

The sense of comradeship, warmth and friendship of the Three of Cups has gone stale, flat and dull. The fourth cup in the image is being offered to the figure beneath the tree, but he does not see it. It is at times like this when we close in on ourselves, put up the barriers, shut the curtains, retreat from the world and withhold feelings or even thoughts.

This is when we are at our most introverted, and can, ironically, be hugely creative if we are conscious of our motivations for being so. The problem is, unless we see it as a chance for enlightenment, psychological insight or self-healing, we often lose the point and think only of our losses, see only our sorrows and thus lose any chance of relating to ourselves.

When you draw this card, don't take everything personally. Don't feel you are the only one who hurts, the only one to blame, the only one who isn't loved. Your life may seem dull and uninteresting; you may feel washed along the shore and that you can't make an effort to do anything, feel anything or care for anyone else. This apathy suggests you are emotionally stuck, that right now you need to open your eyes and see what is offered to you; that soon you will be able to focus on your goals and good feelings will return if you make the effort.

But no one can do it for you. Take time to reflect, but do so in a positive way. Knowing what you want is the first step toward getting it, so examine, evaluate, and don't fear your widening vision. As a "blockage" card, it signifies that you are so defensive and self-absorbed right now that you cannot consider someone's offer or proposal. As a "future" card, be aware that some serious self-reflection is necessary, but with honesty and positive focus you can restore the balance.

Five of Cups

KEY WORDS

Loss, disappointment, emotional confusion, regret

KEY PHRASES

- *Feeling deprived of love*
- *Having something taken away from you*
- *Feeling sad and grieving*
- *Regrets over lost opportunities*
- *Change in priorities*
- *Acceptance of what is*
- *Emotional resistance to change*
- *Wishing you could change the past*
- *Emotional imbalance*

Interpretation

The subject of loss is one we don't handle very easily. This card seems negative in its associations, but there is a positive interpretation to loss, too. Again it is our projection of our fears or doubts that cause us to take this card as a bad penny when it comes up in any reading.

Rather like "Death," this card suggests that it is timely to let go of your attachments, to not fear the loss of one thing, which will soon be replaced by another. It invites you to embrace change and go with the flow. The actual loss may be something as trivial as losing a key, or, more significantly, may signal the loss of a dream, opportunity or a relationship.

The emotions that run with loss are sadness, denial and control. If you draw this card in a "you now" position, you will probably know immediately what it is you regret, have lost or are about to lose. Do you wish you could turn the clock back, long for what might have been or think you made the wrong choice? Look at the figure on the card. He's so focused on the three overturned cups, representing the idea of loss, that he has not noticed the two standing cups, representing new insights and opportunities.

As a "blockage" card, this may indicate that you are so obsessed with your loss you cannot see what is to be gained. Remember, we live in a dualistic world, and for every apparent negative quality there is a positive polarity. Try to see through the "bad" and "good" phenomena of our perception and realize that loss is gain; rather like yin and yang, they are, in fact, one.

As a "future" card, you must acknowledge your mistakes or allow yourself to grieve, and realize that you will soon get back into the flow of your own life stream.

Six of Cups

KEY WORDS

Innocence, nostalgia, playfulness, childhood

KEY PHRASES

- *Acknowledge your inner child*
- *Goodwill to all*
- *Having nostalgic feelings*
- *Sentimental memories*
- *Playful relationship*
- *Naive and innocent*
- *Sharing and reconciliation*

Interpretation

Two children are blissfully involved in the giving and receiving of a cup full of flowers. This card indicates that your inner child is now at work and needs expression. Perhaps it is time to look back to the good childhood memories, to remember how it was to play without all the fears, self-doubt and illusions that you now carry as an adult.

This state of innocence is, of course, colored by many different meanings. But drawing this card suggests nostalgic moments, fond memories, a sense of playfulness that is often lost on the road to maturity.

However, if you draw the Six of Cups as a "blockage" card, you are living too much in the past, probably naively assuming that you don't have to take responsibility for your choices and all will be well. As a "future" card, you will be sharing in the goodwill of others, and also giving out good intentions.

The spirit of this card is all sweetness and light, and, however cynically we can remind ourselves that there is also anger, hatred and violence in this world, generosity and forgiveness also have their place. The Six of Cups implies that by giving out goodness around you it will come back to you, too.

Enjoy feeling playful, and let this card remind you of relationships that have enriched your life as well as those that have been painful. If you have unfinished business from the past, now is the time to put it aside and welcome fulfillment or true exchanges of love in your life.

Seven of Cups

KEY WORDS

*Wishful thinking,
self-indulgence,
too much choice*

KEY PHRASES

- *Feeling disorganized*
- *Fantasizing about what
  you can achieve*
- *High expectations*
- *Lazy attitude to life*
- *Putting off the inevitable*
- *Believing you can get
  away with anything*
- *Having your cake and
  eating it*
- *Illusions about love*
- *An array of options
  open to you*

Interpretation

This card has three very distinct meanings. The first is
that you have so many options that you can't organize
yourself to make the right choice. The second is that you
are living under some kind of illusion about what you can
achieve. The third that you are simply indulging in all kinds
of excesses, or opting for a lazy, sloppy kind of lifestyle.

When you draw this card in the "you now" position, think
honestly about the different meanings. You might be
overwhelmed by thoughts and choices, and not know where
to turn. You might be literally fantasizing about your
abilities or have grand illusions about love. It could be that
too much wishful thinking means you've just given up on
yourself. If, however, you are working all the hours in the day, are totally
disciplined and efficiency personified, then maybe it is time to let go a little.
Indulge in yourself, drop the order and opt for a little laid-back living.

As a "blockage" card, either your illusions and fantasies are preventing you
from moving on or the possibilities before you seem so endless that you daren't
make a personal decision.

As a "future" card, watch out for falling into any of the above traps. On a
positive note, though, it will soon be time to face those options, make your
choice and commit yourself to those plans, rather than avoiding the challenge.
It is all about making your bed, and then lying in it. In a relationship issue,
take care that you do not overestimate what someone has to offer you.

Eight of Cups

KEY WORDS
*Changing direction,
moving on*

KEY PHRASES
- *Commitment to new
  values*
- *Exploring a different
  lifestyle*
- *Leaving behind a
  difficult situation*
- *Walking away from
  the past*
- *A journey of self-
  discovery*
- *Looking for spiritual
  or emotional truth*
- *Realizing it is time
  to start afresh*
- *Moving on to better
  things*

Interpretation

The Eight of Cups signifies a time of transition. This is a period or cycle in your life that means you must move on, move away, follow a new direction or reevaluate your priorities in life.

In the "you now" position, this card suggests that there is an imbalance in your life. Look at the cups in the image. Eight is easily divided into two groups of four, to create a balance, but the cups are stacked in piles of three and five. This suggests that, however much we believe we are in a harmonious situation, job, relationship or place, there is something not quite right about it. If we look ahead, beyond and explore other options, we can restore the balance to our "eightness," in other words, our ability to overcome obstacles.

There is nothing permanent in life except change itself, and this card reminds you that everything moves on or away. People leave us; we leave people; a position of power is taken from you; you take up someone else's position of power. All is interchangeable and this card signifies you have arrived at such an interchange in your life. The signpost may not be clear but, if you explore the deeper meaning behind current events, feelings or fears, you will be able to find a more balanced perspective of your own personal truth.

Strike out on a new route, take a different turning, and accept that change is beneficial. Most of us don't like change—it provokes great anxiety because we feel secure with what we know and trust. This card often raises the question about leaving a relationship, getting out of a rut or just moving on because it is destructive or noncreative for you right now.

In the "blockage" position, it is your very fear of moving on that is creating difficult circumstances for you. In the "future" position, you will soon have to focus on your life direction, whether to find new emotional or spiritual values or to leave the past behind you.

Nine of Cups

KEY WORDS

*Wish fulfillment,
emotional satisfaction,
sensuality, pleasure*

KEY PHRASES

- *Wishes coming true*
- *Sexual satisfaction*
- *Enjoying the simple
  pleasures of life*
- *Pleased with what you
  have achieved*
- *Smugly content*
- *Emotionally satiated*
- *Self-indulgence*
- *Counting your blessings*

Interpretation

Traditionally, this card was known as the "wish card." Your wish will now come true! But take care that you accept the responsibility of that wish and know what you really want. We often think we want something or someone and then live to regret it afterward.

But generally this card is very beneficial, giving you the chance to take pride in your achievements, to be glad for what you are doing, or to feeling sneakily a little bit smug about pulling off your "tour de force." The man in the picture is content; he is almost saying "hey, look at all my cups, bet you haven't got that many!" Caution is required that you don't bask so much in your own success that you close yourself off to others or cause others to envy you. Remember, envy breeds resentment, distorted love and emotional manipulation.

In the "blockage" position, you are so full of yourself and your achievements that you can't see anyone else's point of view. Alternatively, it is your very self-indulgence that is stopping you from making your wish come true.

As a "future" card, you can expect sensual pleasure, sexual satisfaction and feeling like the cat that's got the cream. In fact, the chances are stacked in your favor that your current dream will come true. But, as the saying goes, "don't count your chickens before they've hatched."

Ten of Cups

KEY WORDS

Family happiness, joy, peace, harmony, promise of more to come, safe haven

KEY PHRASES

- *Feeling at one with the world*
- *Seeing the light*
- *Emotional fulfillment*
- *Completion of cycle*
- *Sexual commitment*
- *Love's ideals attainable*
- *Restoring the status quo*

Interpretation

The Ten of Cups indicates that the joy you seek is within reach. Whether it is in family values, a sense of being at one with the world or emotional fulfillment in a relationship, this is a time to count your blessings and prepare for the good times. Just don't become complacent.

The rather sentimental image of a family gazing in awe at a rainbow of cups speaks to our highest ideals. We search for happiness, and draw tarot cards to provide us with some meaning of what is happening to us right now and what is to come.

When you draw this card in the "you now" position, the flow of energy is positive, so make the most of it. Work hard for peace and commitment, love the one you're with and iron out any difficulties. There is a sense of harmony inside you as well as without which will rub off on those close to you. The key to the happiness door might be right in front of your eyes; or your nearest and dearest, lover, family and friends are all there to support you.

As a "blockage" card, you may be so compelled to find love and harmony solely through family values that you are ignoring your own personal pathway. Alternatively, turning your back on the world and idealizing about a "happy ever after" future is preventing you from moving on. In a "future" position, you will soon see the light, welcome emotional fulfillment and restore the balance in your life.

Page of Cups

KEY WORDS

Sensitivity, intimacy, romantic feelings

KEY PHRASES

- *Showing your feelings*
- *Being offered love or romance*
- *Trusting in your intuition*
- *A younger, imaginative lover*
- *Creative ideas*
- *A lighthearted and flirtatious admirer*
- *Daydreaming*
- *Beginning of a love affair*
- *Finding it in your heart to forgive*

Interpretation

Like all the Pages, the Page of Cups indicates a youthful energy, that of love at its most romantic or idealized. This card can signify a new lover coming into your life; young, imaginative, perhaps a little naive, but highly sensitive. Sensitivity, however, can be destructive; the person may only be sensitive to his or her own needs and desires, forgetting those of the object of their affection, so take care.

However much this Page seems to represent the lighthearted and flirtatious encounter that we seek in our daily lives, the idea of such refined courtly love comes with a price. Once the ideals of the early days of romance have faded, once you see beyond the image of the perfect lover you have projected onto someone, then the disillusionment can hurt.

But do take this card to show the beginnings of emotional sensitivity at its most positive. Interaction in this kind of relationship swings from high to low, obsession, moods, emotional confusion and sexual intimacy. If you are already involved in a relationship, then this card indicates that it is time to be more sensitive to your own and your partner's needs, and to be more creative with the relationship.

As a "blockage" card, think about what you have to offer in a current relationship. What has your lover got to offer? And perhaps one of you is so sensitive to your own feelings that you are immune to your partner's.

As a "future" card, expect to encounter romance, new conquests or lighthearted intimacy. You are given the go-ahead to flirt and play romantically, as long as you don't fall into the traps suggested above.

Knight of Cups

KEY WORDS

Idealization, emotional sensitivity, in love with love, invitation to love, romantic overflow, temperamental

KEY PHRASES

- *Knight in shining armor*
- *Emotional rescue*
- *Dashing off to rescue someone*
- *Exaggeration of feeling*
- *Melancholic but then ecstatic*
- *Loves beauty but hates imperfection*
- *Imaginative but unrealistic*
- *Gushing sentiments, suspect intentions*

Interpretation

Whether you are the "knight in shining armor" yourself or
the victim who needs to be rescued, you should check
that your intentions, well-meaning or welcoming, are
not an illusion. This card often turns up in a layout when
we are not being honest about our feelings. So think
about what your role is within a relationship. Do you
want to be rescued or does the object of your desire want
to be rescued?

Genuine self-questioning is always necessary with all the Knight cards
because they represent the extremes of their suit's energy. On the positive side,
when drawn as a "you now" or "future" card, this represents someone who is a
great lover, is full of emotions, charm and desire to please the other.

On the negative side, the Knight of Cups suggests someone who is even
more sensitive to the atmosphere and opinions of others than the Page. They
"take things personally," but are immune to others' feelings, they get twitchy,
petulant, irritable and melodramatic about life.

If in the "blockage" position, this card may represent an aspect of yourself.
Learn to recognize if the energy is helping you or hindering you in some way.
Ask yourself the following questions: Are you in love with love, not the real
person? Are your feelings genuine or romantically out of all proportion? Can
you bear rows and scenes or do you run away to hide in the bathroom if
someone raises their voice or expresses their anger?

Also think about whether the Knight's energy is missing in your life. Are
you in need of emotional rescue, is life dull and static, is your partner slumped
on the sofa every night? Is it time to open up, be more sensitive, play a
romantic game, indulge in the most fanciful and protean of love's experience?
Pure romance. Are your intentions idealized?

Queen of Cups

KEY WORDS
Empathy, tenderhearted, emotionally aware, compassionate

KEY PHRASES
- *Unconditional love*
- *Kindness and understanding*
- *Emotional harmony*
- *Know what it feels like to feel*
- *Aware of emotional undercurrents*
- *Patient and calm*
- *Willing to help the underdog*

Interpretation

The Queen of Cups indicates that emotional understanding has a high priority in your life right now or will have in the near future. But you have the resources necessary to understand how others feel, empathize with any difficult situation, give your support and love generously and unconditionally.

In the "you now" position, you are so full of compassion that you will draw like-minded souls to you, or those who seek your good nature and respect. Alternatively, the Queen of Cups can represent someone, either man or woman, who is in your life and can help you to work positively with your feelings. They are waiting for you to open up.

As a "blockage" card, the Queen of Cups asks you to consider whether you are too emotionally involved with someone to see the truth. Or that you are so willing to commit yourself to helping or loving someone that you are repressing your own emotional needs.

As a "future" card, you will soon have to let go of any resentments or anger and be more compassionate with yourself and others. Someone who represents all the Queen's tenderhearted qualities could also be an important signpost in the next step of your personal journey. Don't dismiss those qualities; they lead to greater self-awareness and tolerance of others.

King of Cups

KEY WORDS

Stability, wisdom, diplomacy, generosity, support

KEY PHRASES

- *Emotional security*
- *Awareness of human nature*
- *A wise person*
- *Accepting one's limitations*
- *Keeping your head in a crisis*
- *Acting from controlled emotion rather than instinct*
- *Evaluating the situation*
- *Creating a balanced atmosphere*

Interpretation

The King of Cups indicates that wisdom, emotional maturity and guidance are important energies in your life right now. It is that stability represented by the phrase "if you can keep your head, when all about you are losing theirs," combined with a calm approach to current events, which will see you through any confusions.

In the "you now" position, this card reflects your ability to get a job done properly, or that you are aware of the facts, and that tolerance and self-discipline will create the change you seek. Alternatively, a new stabilizing force, perhaps a man or woman in authority, is having a powerful influence over you for the better. They offer wisdom and security, and can give good advice.

In a relationship issue, you are now at a point where emotional maturity enables you to be creative within that relationship. You are relaxed, you keep cool, you see the value in keeping your perspective, and even smile a little at the world and its idiosyncrasies.

As a "blockage" card, you may be controlling your emotions to such an extent that you cannot express the truth of your desires and feelings. Or a mature person is using emotional blackmail or knowledge to control you. It is time to open up and focus on real wisdom, which comes from acceptance and awareness of your strengths and weaknesses and being able to work with them.

As a "future outcome" card, you will be blessed with a calm perspective on human nature, or give good advice to someone and be able to evaluate the roles that are played within relationships in order to make decisions accordingly. Alternatively, you will meet someone who represents all these qualities and who will have a specific role to play in the issue that needs to be resolved.

Suit of Swords

Swords, associated with the element Air, represent the rational and logical way we make decisions in life, yet the images and traditional associations attached to this suit seem incredibly bleak. What can this mean?

There is a myth that logic and reason are the only way to fight our own inner battles. If we reason with our emotions and rationalize away our desires, we will sort out all our problems. Ironically, the suit of Swords indicates that our rational minds have led us astray, often far away from the truth.

We have illusions, we have ideals, we have principles, and it is these illusions that the Swords "cut through." We must use objectivity and rationalize or analyze what is going on, but we must also accept another kind of "knowing." We must learn to rely on our inner voice, to trust and connect with the source within us.

Swords are "double-edged" indeed. They remind us that our deceptions, illusions and fears are the very "demons" that need to be faced, and that the "logical" and rational must work with the wisdom of our heart.

KEY WORDS

Thought, the mind, information, connection, ideals, self-expression

Suit of Swords exercise

Before looking up each interpretation for the suit of Swords, try this exercise to help you get to know the cards.

1 Lay the court cards face up toward you in ascending order—Page, Knight, Queen, King.

2 Look at the different images on the court cards. Can you identify with these people or do you know people who are like them? For example, one of the positive attributes of the Queen is someone who gets straight to the point.

3 Next think about yourself. Are you logical? Do you analyze situations or use your instinct? Do the gloomier images alarm you, or do you instantly turn off or rationalize them?

4 Now lay out the numbered cards and look at the different images. Most of the numbered cards are people *alone* in the world. They are not aware of what's going on around them, only thinking of themselves. The cards represent our sense of *conscious separation* from the rest of the world, our existential loneliness, so always interpret them as the chance to get to the truth of the matter.

Ace of Swords

KEY WORDS

Clarity, truth, objectivity, honesty, justice

KEY PHRASES

- *Cutting through illusion*
- *Realizing the way forward*
- *Using logic and facing the facts*
- *Establishing what is right and wrong*
- *Facing up to reality*
- *Analyzing your motives*
- *Mental adroitness*

Interpretation

Something needs expression when you see the Ace of Swords, whether it is an idea, a home truth, a spot of self-honesty or a need for justice. But, whatever it is, you may not recognize it at first.

This card also represents facing up to any new challenge with logic and firmness. Believe in yourself, don't doubt your motivations or intentions, be ready to leap into action, and be objective about your limitations.

The Ace of Swords says face the facts and don't carry bitterness and disillusion from the past because otherwise you won't be able to move forward. This is a card of fortitude and resolution, but it means you need to be as honest with yourself as you can be. If you can clear the air, dispense with doubt and confusion, the way will be clear to you. There may be a problem that you have to resolve and life is never smooth, but now is the time to analyze the situation and get cracking.

If this card appears in a "blockage" position, you are letting your head totally overrule your heart or gut instinct. Too much analysis is blinding you to the truth of the matter, and you need to engage your feelings in the issue as well as your brain cells.

As a "future" card, the Ace of Swords suggests that there is a challenge coming soon, but out of that challenge you can make something better of your life. The opportunities coming your way may require more effort on your part, but they will open you to new possibilities and success.

Two of Swords

KEY WORDS
Denial, blocked feelings, repressed emotions

KEY PHRASES
- *Blind to the truth,*
- *Pretending one thing, feeling another*
- *Being cool and unavailable*
- *Denying your feelings*
- *Defensive attitude*
- *Ignoring the truth*
- *Blocking out others*
- *Putting up barriers*
- *Being unwilling to make a choice*

Interpretation

The woman in the image has raised a barrier around her heart, she is blindfolded and lets nothing in and nothing out. In fact, she denies not only her own self-expression but also that of others.

The Two of Swords tells us about the way we deny we have feelings, pretend indifference, avoid the truth of our emotions and refuse to feel them. We split off our feelings, put them in containers, hope they will go away or rot slowly in our psychological basement so that we don't have to deal with them. When we are in denial of our feelings, we refuse to acknowledge they exist. We say things like "What do you mean, unhappy? I'm never unhappy, let me tell you a joke."

This card also refers to the repression of feelings—when we say to ourselves: "No, I mustn't express my anger, it's too dangerous to let it all out, I might hurt someone or myself."

If you draw the Two of Swords in the "you now" position, perhaps you are avoiding your feelings or won't accept the truth about a situation. Ask yourself: Do you have any feelings? Are you squashing them, blocking out others? Are you fearful of being hurt? Are you actually raging inside but telling jokes on the outside? Are you blind to your situation through choice, or necessity?

As a "blockage" card, the Two of Swords suggests you are cut off not only from yourself, but from someone else. And what you need to learn right now is to open up, drop the guard, let down the drawbridge and not fear the truth.

Three of Swords

KEY WORDS

wounding, disbelief, rejection

KEY PHRASES

- *Getting to the heart of the matter*
- *Triumph of logic over emotion*
- *Torn between two lovers*
- *Feeling hurt inside*
- *Discovering a painful truth*
- *Feeling let down*
- *Feeling others are out to hurt you*
- *Being cheated on*
- *Fear of losing your partner*
- *Jealous imaginings*
- *Wanting to hurt someone emotionally*

Interpretation

The Three of Swords has a variety of meanings, and, like any double-edged sword, you must try to apply the interpretation to your current situation with complete emotional honesty.

The positive side of this card is that with a clear head, an open mind and acceptance of your feelings you can get to the heart of any situation and sort it out. But it does require complete self-awareness.

Commonly, this card tends to be biased toward its more "negative" interpretations. When we feel let down in love, betrayed and emotionally hurt, our world suddenly seems unjust and we are heartbroken or fearful of losing someone. All these experiences have something in common, and that is that we suffer alone, thinking that we are the only one to feel these feelings, and we believe no one has ever felt what we feel. Good old logic and reason seem to be the last things that would save us. But, if you examine your issues with care, talk to others, and realize that your pain is someone else's pain, it can lead to a better understanding of yourself and others.

Often these feelings are based on reality, but sometimes they are based on irrational fear. This is where jealousy often rears its head; jealousy stemming from a deep-seated fear of rejection. We often assume that if someone isn't possessive or jealous of us then maybe that person doesn't really love us at all.

When you draw the Three of Swords, in whatever position, take a reality check. Are you jealous of your partner for no reason? Are they jealous of you? What is your deepest fear when you draw this card? Could it be the fear of rejection and loneliness?

Four of Swords

KEY WORDS

Repose, temporary retreat, contemplation, truce, inner fears, emotional ghosts from the past

KEY PHRASES

- *Making time for yourself to be alone*
- *Finding your own space*
- *Relaxing and taking it easy*
- *Standing back and reviewing the situation*
- *Preparing for the future*
- *Taking stock of your objectives*
- *Slowing down*

Interpretation

The Four of Swords has two distinct interpretations when in the "you now" position: first, that our own past prevents us from moving on. We feel stuck, paralyzed by our fears and self-doubt generated by failures, pains, disappointments or betrayals of the past. It is important to look at these fears in the cold light of day and they will soon disappear.

The second interpretation is that confrontation with others is not appropriate right now. Instead of rushing in to make a decision or forcing an issue, stand back, retreat, find time to think things through or contemplate the true nature of your current situation.

Is it as important as you think it is? Are you exaggerating your desires, or assuming too much? As soon as you have achieved clarity within yourself, you can then focus on the issue at stake.

If you have a relationship question, this card implies that a break away from each other or more space will allow you to see your relationship from a more objective perspective.

The Four of Swords also indicates that it is time to be more conscious about any unspoken agreements in your relationship. We often have hidden agendas in our relationships and deny that we have unresolved problems or feelings. Sometimes we have to speak up or our lives become a frozen wasteland. Take care if you get this card in the "blockage" position that this isn't the case. Constructive communication may be needed right now.

As a future card, you will need to take a step back, have a break or find some peace and quiet to prepare yourself for new events or experiences.

Five of Swords

KEY WORDS

Conquest, defeat, hollow victory, accepting limitations, conflicting interests

KEY PHRASES

- *No-win situation*
- *Thinking of yourself and no one else*
- *Winning the battle*
- *Feeling defeated*
- *Dishonorable behavior*
- *Experiencing hostility*

Interpretation

The meaning of the Five of Swords has always been controversial and rather confused in tarot circles. Some readers tend to look at it as a sign of retreat, and that the questioner is represented by one of the two forlorn characters rather than the victorious one. So accepting your limitations and acknowledging a sense of defeat is the most common interpretation for this card.

However, I believe it also implies that you have conquered your fears or won a fair battle in spite of the odds against you. Again, all this depends on your personal perspective and whether are you projecting negative or positive qualities onto the card.

As a "you now" card, both of the above interpretations can apply, but equally it is timely to question your own self-interest. Ask yourself the following questions: Am I putting my interests over and above everyone else's? What is so important to me that I have to prove everyone else is wrong?

Alternatively, this card can also imply that it is time to put yourself first but to be aware of hollow victories. Interpreting this card isn't hard if you accept that you will project your current reaction to "conquest" and "defeat" onto the card. You will either see yourself as the loser turning away and having to accept that you can't always win, or see yourself as the winner who also has to accept that sometimes you will lose. Both are about acceptance of limitations.

As a "blockage" card, however, the Five of Swords suggests that there is conflict or hostility in your life, someone is playing power games and there are dishonorable feelings out there, possibly your own.

As a "future" card, the Five of Swords means you will encounter hostility, feel that you must either win or lose, and learn to accept that others have boundaries and limits, too.

The Minor Arcana

Six of Swords

KEY WORDS

New perspective, recovery, travel

KEY PHRASES

- *Moving away from trouble*
- *Getting over difficulties*
- *Heading on to better times*
- *Having to change location*
- *Mental or physical journey*
- *Leaving the past behind*
- *Beginning to be more positive about life*

Interpretation

If you feel you are in troubled waters right now, then this card indicates that you are about to move into calmer ones, particularly if the card is in the "you now" position. You are not exactly exuberant and you are a little wary of what's ahead, but you can at last see life or events with a more objective perspective. You are moving ahead or moving away from circumstances that were uncomfortable or uncertain, and now you can see the way forward.

When this card is in the "blockage" position, you may be feeling apathetic, life doesn't seem to be flowing, and you are lost or depressed. But just keeping your head above water won't get you results, nor will thinking "if only I'd done X instead of Y." It's time to free yourself from past troubles and fears and to accept that two rights won't make a wrong.

As a "future" card, the Six of Swords suggests that soon you will be rowing away from the choppy waters of turmoil and taking a much easier route.

The Six of Swords is also linked to a readiness to communicate and exchange ideas, particularly in a relationship question. It suggests that you need to merge your different perspectives and get to know your partner better by understanding how they tick. If you exchange ideas, you must also see the other person's viewpoint. The Six of Swords signifies that mutual consciousness and cooperation will help you solve any current problems.

Seven of Swords

KEY WORDS
Dishonesty, subterfuge, stealth, deception

KEY PHRASES
- *Running away from the truth*
- *Avoiding responsibility*
- *Keeping a secret to yourself*
- *Wanting to be a loner*
- *Not facing the music*
- *Manipulative behavior*
- *Lying or cheating*
- *Self-deception or fooling others*

Interpretation

Whenever you see the Seven of Swords, don't run away from the truth of this card! A man is seen stealthily running away with some swords, sure that no one has spotted him; he is obviously up to something very secretive and possibly dishonest.

When you draw this card in the "you now" position, it is likely that you aren't facing the truth. Perhaps you don't want to face the music or you are avoiding obligations such as work, a relationship issue or some kind of commitment.

There may be dishonest people around you, someone who may be trying to deceive you in some way, a trickster, sneak and liar. A friend or lover could be two-faced, you could claim credit for something you didn't do or someone is complaining behind your back.

The Seven of Swords also says: "Look behind, have you covered your tracks, are you sure no one is going to point the finger of blame at you later?" It might be something you have done that you'd rather not admit, but it could be for the good of others or simply yourself, but can you get away with it?

Perhaps you are embarking on a new love affair and escaping an old one; whatever you are up to, are you deceiving yourself that this is the right action to take? Try to use the ideal of the Swords, logic and clarity to get to the truth and clear the air. Sometimes isolating yourself from others can be an enormous burden; look at the very solitary nature of the thief on the card who will have to take responsibility for his actions.

As a "blockage" position card, the Seven of Swords indicates that you are simply making things worse for yourself by not facing up to the truth.

Eight of Swords

KEY WORDS

Restriction, self-sabotage, isolation, vulnerability

KEY PHRASES

- *Feeling fenced in*
- *Lack of freedom to choose*
- *Feeling trapped and bound by a situation*
- *Waiting to be rescued*
- *Scattered ideas and no direction*
- *Feeling powerless or victimized*
- *Floundering in feeling*
- *Bound by your illusions*

Interpretation

Notice that most of the key phrases for the Eight of Swords are about "feeling." Yet it is our concepts, ideas, mentality and thoughts that bind us to our feelings and, in turn, create those very personal dilemmas and problems. The woman on the card could easily free herself if she made the effort, but it is almost as if she is sabotaging her chances to move on by remaining restricted because it's easier to do so.

As a "blockage" card, it implies that it is hard work to wriggle out of those ropes, to struggle through the swords of illusion, and often easier to flounder in a state of vulnerability in the hope that someone will come and along and rescue us.

But this card suggests that you need to focus and to find clarity, rather than assume you will find someone to rescue your from your victimized feelings. Unfortunately, no one can rescue us from ourselves, solutions aren't easy, but they are there, and if you open yourself to possibilities you won't have to play the victim either.

Alternatively, the Eight of Swords signifies that you are restricted by "real" events, perhaps stuck in a codependent relationship, a boring job, no job, not enough money. These are very "real" events for us and we feel trapped, confused and unable to shift.

If you draw this card in a "you now" position, then take it that you are already feeling restricted either by some difficult experience or by your own lack of direction. Either way, the other cards in the layout will give you clues as to how to deal with this current mud bath. Remember, you do have choices and there is a way out if you use the power of objectivity and clear thinking. Free yourself from your troubles by letting go of the concepts or ideas to which you are attached.

Nine of Swords

KEY WORDS

Guilt, worry, overwhelmed by feelings

KEY PHRASES

- *Overburdened by thoughts*
- *Feeling you have done something wrong*
- *Wishing "if only"*
- *Regretting the past*
- *Sleepless nights*
- *Obsessive sorrow*
- *Feeling vulnerable*

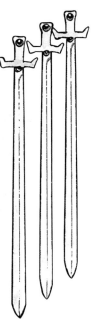

Interpretation

Although this card appears to be one of the bleakest of the suit of Swords, it carries the positive message that the darkest hour comes just before the dawn. We can rise and see the light of day from the depths of despair and our greatest fears and woes. We all have nights when we toss and turn, our thoughts get out of proportion, we blame ourselves, blame others, worry about our actions and flounder in our doubts.

If you draw this card in a "you now" position, it is time to think logically about why you feel worried, why you may feel guilty for something or just why you are unhappy. This card can also mean that you need to search deeper within yourself to root out the cause of these nagging thoughts. Sometimes we feel "there's something wrong, but I can't put my finger on it." The Nine of Swords is pushing you to wake up to what that is.

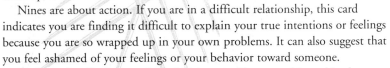

Nines are about action. If you are in a difficult relationship, this card indicates you are finding it difficult to explain your true intentions or feelings because you are so wrapped up in your own problems. It can also suggest that you feel ashamed of your feelings or your behavior toward someone.

Explore what illusions are immobilizing you if you get this card in the "blockage" position. Alternatively, are you so overwhelmed by nagging problems or worrying about everyone else that you can't make headway with your plans? Accept that you do have a vulnerable spot, and that it's time to be honest about your Achilles' heel and work with your mistakes or bad feelings constructively.

The Nine of Swords basically reminds you that it is time to refocus your goals, because just a little tweak here and there could make a big difference.

Ten of Swords

KEY WORDS

Enlightenment, turning point, martyrdom

KEY PHRASES

- *Exaggerated self-pity*
- *Feeling life is against you*
- *Playing the victim*
- *Cutting through illusions*

Interpretation

Always a rather alarming card to draw in a layout, the Ten of Swords isn't as bad as it looks. There are differing interpretations of the Ten of Swords, because it is one of the most powerful and complex cards in the deck, but, like all tens, this card indicates the end of a cycle and the beginning of a new one. But before you can embark on a new journey you must liberate yourself from old patterns of behavior, drop emotional baggage and say good-bye to the "old you." It's time to declutter your life.

In this sense the Ten of Swords represents enlightenment; it is timely now to accept your illusions for what they are. Even if you are feeling "disillusioned," this can only lead to a new self-awareness. Right now you must look forward and put the past behind you.

In the "you now" position, this card indicates that you've reached a turning point when things just can't get any worse. Everyone seems to be against you, you mope about how unfair life is and bemoan your fate. But it is often at this point when you've gone down into the depths that you must realize that the only way is up and out again.

In the "blockage" position, it can indicate that you are exaggerating your problems, and that they are not as bad as you make out. Or you may be playing the victim or martyr to wield a certain amount of power over someone. In a relationship issue, the script that springs to mind would be you reminding your partner of what you've had to suffer: "Look at what I've given up for you!"; or "No, it's fine, I don't need anyone, I can do it alone." The power of the victim and martyr are equally chilling in their manifestation.

As a future card, prepare for a change of heart, be ready to face the new you, and laugh a little at the world and its coincidences. If you truly are suffering, then this card really does indicate a turn for the better.

Page of Swords

KEY WORDS

Vigilance, ready for action, logic and reason, mental dexterity

KEY PHRASES

- *Wisdom based on experience*
- *Communicate your plans*
- *Research the facts*
- *Youthful ideas*
- *Refreshing honesty*
- *A young-at-heart person*
- *Challenging lover*

Interpretation

When you draw the Page of Swords as a "you now" card, you are ready for the challenges to come. They might not be the ones you particularly want, but you are vigilant and prepared for the next stage of any situation. With foresight and logic you can communicate your ideas and work out the best way to deal with any test or challenge.

You need to provoke a challenge, so that you can prove you have mental courage. Be honest about your needs or desires and look at all the facts. When you see this card, consider whether you fear challenges or whether you welcome them. Are you like the Page of Swords, ready to stand up for yourself, to show you are honest and truthful, or more likely to turn your head?

Challenges come in many forms. Sword challenges are about questions, problems or tasks that stimulate your mind, perhaps even an invitation to engage in a contest of wills in a relationship. The word "vigilance" is rooted in a Latin word that means "to keep awake." The Page of Swords reminds you to open your eyes, see the truth, don't let emotional fears swamp you and use the positive qualities of the Swords. Those include the spirit of learning, communication and objective thinking to see your way forward.

If this appears as a "blockage" card, stop deceiving yourself that you know all the answers. Sometimes you must question and challenge yourself, too.

Knight of Swords

KEY WORDS

Self-assured, incisive, frank, impetuous, knowledgeable, critical or indiscreet, impatient, tactless and brusque, powerful intellect

KEY PHRASES

• *Analyzes the situation*
• *Cuts off from feeling*

Interpretation

Like all the Knights, our chevalier of the Swords represents the extremes of the suit's energy. When this card appears in a layout, take care which energy you identify with. The Knight either represents an aspect of yourself or someone you know.

As a "you now" card, use your energy positively to analyze the current situation, but don't rush headlong into making any decisions without careful thought. You may want to get things done hastily, you may lack sensitivity or simply be so influential and intellectually together that you know you can persuade anyone to see things your way.

The vain assumptions of the Knight might manifest via others. A partner may be aloof or emotionally distant, or rush headlong into a new project without thinking of the consequences. A friend or new admirer might demand too much attention or is tactless, gets straight to the point or won't take no for an answer.

The Knight of Swords can also imply that you need to be more self-assured, speak up, not fear criticism or worry that you are going to upset someone by what you believe. Remember, when you draw a Knight, you must apply your current situation or issue to the layout. Be very honest about which extreme of behavior the knight of Swords is representing in your life.

In a "blockage" position, you may be letting your head rule your heart or someone is so authoritarian or overbearing in their viewpoint that you don't have a chance to speak up about your own needs.

Queen of Swords

KEY WORDS

No-nonsense, astute, unpretentious, direct, realistic and straightforward

KEY PHRASES

- *Gets to the point*
- *Up-front and open*
- *Honest and quick-witted*
- *Lively intellect*
- *Strong character*
- *Suppressed emotions*
- *Judgmental person*

Interpretation

This Queen has made it to the throne because of her ability to see quickly how to resolve problems. She is a fast thinker, she is shrewd and she is realistic about what can be achieved and what is best avoided.

If you draw this card in a "you now" position, then you may well identify with her positive attributes of being direct and to the point. It is your intellectual knowledge and astute way of looking at the situation that will get you results.

But, like all Sword cards, the Queen has a negative association, too, particularly if in a "blockage" position. For example, it is fine being up-front and direct or the witty, perceptive authority on life, but it can also mean you could be suppressing your true emotional needs. Alternatively, you find fault with everything and everyone around you because no one can live up to your high expectations. Ask yourself whether you are assessing a situation, person or experience from a truly objective viewpoint or not.

This card can also indicate someone in your life who embodies both the positive and negative qualities listed above; perhaps someone who seems to be an authority on life, astute, clever and savvy. But what does their presence in your life mean? Is it perhaps to inspire you to be like them? To evoke the realization that if you express your logical side tempered with a healthy dose of realism, then you will be able to move on and up? Or that perhaps being so sure of oneself intellectually is often a compensation for a deeper vulnerability that needs to be addressed?

King of Swords

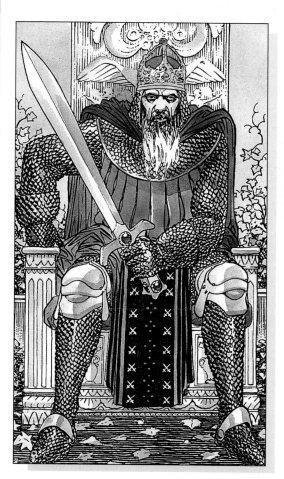

KEY WORDS

Articulate, direct, just, assertive, analytical

KEY PHRASES

- *Actively gets to grips with the situation*
- *Objective outlook on life*
- *Has high standards*
- *Fair judgment*
- *Patriarchal values*
- *Capable and prudent*
- *Intellectually adept*

Interpretation

This King seems sure of himself. He has knowledge and intellect as his armory. He is highly principled. The King of Swords represents the most powerful energy of this suit, that of using the mind to solve problems, to cut through mental confusion and challenge others with ideas.

When you draw this card in the "you now" position, you are ready to handle your affairs in an honorable way. You can see through the fog, get to the heart of the matter, resolve any conflicts through the power of your thoughts. Kings represent "active" energy, so you can pit your wits against others, be challenged but know your ideas are sound, diligently research an issue, or communicate the truth with an impartial viewpoint.

The King of Swords can also indicate someone in your life who embodies these qualities and acts as a catalyst to activate those very qualities in you. It is easy to criticize patriarchal values when feminine attributes are currently more fashionable. We must intuit and feel, go with the flow. And we often feel deep resentment toward people who seemingly wield their intellectual sword, challenge our thoughts or have high principles that no one can live up to. The King of Swords reminds you that intellectual reasoning is as important in your life right now as your feelings. Synthesize any emotional sensitivity with your current ability to articulate and analyze a situation.

As a "blockage" card, the King of Swords suggests you are too assertive, you have blocked out your emotional needs for the sake of dogmatism and intolerance of others. Alternatively, someone in your life is so sure of their viewpoint that you feel intellectually squashed, or they use the power of approval and disapproval to control you.

Suit of Pentacles

Pentacles (also called Discs or Coins) are associated with the Earth and, like the zodiac signs for the element of Earth, represent personal resources and the very substance of our being. They tell us about our talents or lack of them, the apparent concrete world, what makes us feel safe or is reliable and how we can be of service to others and ourselves. This suit also represents those things which define and shape us into who we are.

KEY WORDS
Substance, the senses, reality, the tangible

It could be our identification with work, people, skill, creative talent, or it could be our psychological armory—how secure we feel, what gives us a sense of purpose or defines us in the context of a relationship. We have skin, bones and body mass, this is our physical substance; but we also have psychological and spiritual substance. "Tangible" also relates to how we view the external world from our inner one. Do we have a realistic view of life, do we want wealth or a better connection to nature?

It is easy to describe this suit as merely representing material goods, money and success. But there are two sides to all these coins and it is important to remember that it is our own unique perception of so-called reality that is in question.

Suit of Pentacles exercise

Before looking up each interpretation for the suit of Pentacles, try this exercise to help you get to know the cards.

1 Lay the court cards face up toward you in ascending order—Page, Knight, Queen, King.

2 Do you know people who are like them? For example, the positive attributes of the Queen are nurturing skills and down-to-earth. How do you react to this type of person? Or what about the negative aspects of the Knight, inflexible and reluctant to take a risk? Could this be a side of you, too? Do you identify with these characters easily or not?

3 Lay the number cards out in ascending order. Think about the different images and how you react to each card. Next, think about yourself. Are you creative, do you like structure and organization? Do you have a laid-back outlook on life or an obsessive one? Most of the numbered cards represent people *interacting* with the world, doing things. The suit of Pentacles represents our *sense of connection* to the rest of the world and to our own boundaries.

Ace of Pentacles

KEY WORDS

Reward for effort, prosperity, abundance, realism

KEY PHRASES

- *Practical accomplishment*
- *Tangible results*
- *Power to get what you need*
- *Trusting in the situation*
- *Starting afresh*
- *Turning over a new leaf*
- *Being grounded in the real world*

Interpretation

The materialistic energy of the Ace of Pentacles encourages you to sow those seeds of success, get those projects going and take advantage of what is working for you right now. This is not the time to chase rainbows, but for valid schemes and good follow-through.

If this card appears in the "you now" or "current" position, focus on tangible results and draw on your practical knowledge and skills to invest in yourself and your future. This card, like all of the Aces, represents new beginnings; in this case, one that is down-to-earth, centered and reliable for you as an individual. So act now for good results.

In a "blockage" position, the Ace of Pentacles signifies that you are so focused on material gain or financial potential that you aren't aware of your deeper needs and desires. Being surrounded by the trappings of material security is often the only way we can feel safe because we think we can block the feelings of human vulnerability that flow through all of us.

As a "future outlook" card, you will soon have all the resources at hand to make a success of whatever you intend. Accept what is and enjoy your sense of external and internal well-being. This is not a time to play with fire, it is about getting your hands dirty. But if you tap into this regenerative energy you will feel prosperous and experience both spiritual and psychological growth.

Two of Pentacles

KEY WORDS

Balancing, dexterity, flexibility, juggling

KEY PHRASES

- *Agility in dealing with material things*
- *Adapting to relationship needs*
- *Doing many things simultaneously*
- *Dealing with several problems at once*
- *Feeling confident in your abilities*
- *Having fun*
- *Juggling with the options*
- *Being willing to go with the flow*
- *Understanding change*

Interpretation

The easygoing juggler in the image reminds us
of the infinite possibilities there are in life—
choices, options, new developments,
changing scenarios—and how important
it is to stay flexible and open to change.
This card also signifies that, to overcome
any hurdles or problems, be ready to juggle with all the
options. Have fun and smile at life a little, and look for new ways to
handle old situations. In adapting to the world around you, you will also create
an effective way to achieve your current aims.

In a "you now" position, this card means that you are beginning to have
more confidence in your talents and abilities, and it is time to believe in
yourself. Refuse to let change upset you, stay alert to the things you might have
to balance, both in your relationships and in your working life.

As a "blockage" card, you might be juggling too many things at once, and
need to slow down a bit. Don't overstimulate your mind or body; perhaps you
need to let someone else help balance the psychological books with you. If you
"keep an account" emotionally of the games played between you and someone
else, it could be time to develop a new way of relating.

As a "future" card, expect lively, fun times ahead, navigate life with a little
flexibility and expand your awareness of the flux of change.

Three of Pentacles

KEY WORDS

Skill, cooperation, teamwork, planning

KEY PHRASES

- *Professional growth*
- *Material gain*
- *Proving yourself*
- *A competent strategy*
- *Being aware of your potential*
- *Getting together with others*
- *Team spirit*
- *Recognition of skill*
- *Being obsessed with detail*
- *Too dependent on others' opinions*

Interpretation

On the surface this card seems to signify great
success that comes with planning and
teamwork. What would we do without
the confidence of others? How could
we create a masterpiece if it weren't
for careful planning and competent
colleagues or friends for support?

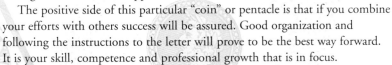

The positive side of this particular "coin" or pentacle is that if you combine
your efforts with others success will be assured. Good organization and
following the instructions to the letter will prove to be the best way forward.
It is your skill, competence and professional growth that is in focus.

However, this card can also indicate that it is up to you to be engaged in a
project or a process that you are totally passionate about, where there is no
ambiguity or ambivalence, and where you can do your own thing without
becoming a mere spoke in the wheel. The latter won't be enough to satisfy you.

In the "blockage" position, you are so obsessed with the details of a project
that you can't see the wood for the trees. Alternatively, you are too dependent
on what others think to go your own way. Seeking approval through your
actions, your "team spirit," might not be all that it seems. Perhaps you need to
be more of an individualist. As a "future" card, assume you will be able to
create the right kind of environment and enterprise for success. Be proud of
what you are about to achieve and revel a little in your own talents or skills.

Four of Pentacles

KEY WORDS

*Mean, possessive, control
freak, stubborn, stagnant*

KEY PHRASES

- *Refusing to budge*
- *Believing your way is
  the only way*
- *Limiting your viewpoint*
- *Controlling others with
  materialism*
- *It's mine!*
- *Resisting change*
- *Tight-fisted and
  mercenary*
- *Small-minded,
  penny-pinching*

Interpretation

You just have to look at the figure in the image to understand its meaning—this is one "mean" individual in the tarot pack. The Four of Pentacles represents, on one level, the world of materialism at its worst. We can all get possessive about what we own. We control our purse strings, can't bear to give away that old CD we never listen to anymore, we control others very subtly through our egos' need to possess and thereby maintain control. We relate to others by defining our territory, saying "this is mine, not yours."

The Four of Pentacles in the "you now" position can suggest that your powerlessness is provoking you to try to control a situation. You believe that your way is the only way over issues concerning money and possessions; or you have a fierce determination to take control of others.

Yet there is also a positive side to the Four of Pentacles. If you are involved in an uncontrollable situation, if a relationship is getting confused or fizzling out, or you are financially strapped, then structure, organization and realistic planning is important now.

As a "blockage" card, someone else might be mean and miserly in your life (but don't forget this could also be a reflection of you); they may be stopping you from making the changes you need to progress. They might control you through possessiveness or manipulate you through financial necessity. As an "outcome" card, you must look carefully at control issues in your relationships and learn to accept that possessiveness is rooted in a fear of change and emotional insecurity.

Five of Pentacles

KEY WORDS

Lack, victim mentality, hardship, rejection

KEY PHRASES

- *Spiritual separation*
- *Soul-searching*
- *Emotionally wounded*
- *Unworthiness*
- *Feeling alone or excluded*
- *Neglecting your needs*
- *A sense that something is missing in your life*

Interpretation

There is always a feeling of "lack" when you draw the Five of Pentacles. It might simply feel like you lack material security on the surface, but there is something deeper at work here. There is a neediness, a feeling that something is missing, whether a spiritual connection or a meaning to life.

This card often appears when we feel emotionally deprived or have become a victim in a relationship. Sometimes it is easier and also more empowering to remain the deprived wanting person in a codependent relationship. This card also signifies that you are lonely, in need of love, feel unworthy of someone's love or are just neglecting yourself physically or emotionally.

The positive side of this card says that, if there is something missing in your life right now, then you must go out and discover what it is. Perhaps you need a spiritual belief, more love, less materialistic dependency or more self-reliance. This is the mentality of someone who sees the glass half empty rather than half full, the pessimist who experiences a sense of rejection or abandonment. Feeling left out in the cold means that it is time to come into the warmth, but you have to take responsibility for doing so yourself.

If you fear asking for help, ask yourself why. Are you too proud, too fearful of opening old wounds, or are you denying your feelings at the expense of material benefit?

As a "blockage" card, this indicates that you may be so wrapped up in your sense of deprivation that you can't see your way forward. The price to be paid for remaining a victim is that someone will always want to save you, but what kind of rescue do you really want? Isn't it better to rescue yourself? This card can also imply a fear (whether unfounded or not) of rejection, whether from a prospective employer, a publisher or a lover.

Six of Pentacles

KEY WORDS

Generosity, willingness, gifts, consideration

KEY PHRASES

- *Loss and gain*
- *Giving and taking*
- *Shift in power*
- *To have and to have not*
- *Domination or submission?*
- *Seeking approval*

Interpretation

It all looks very harmonious on the card; a kindly benefactor is donating his spare cash to one beggar while the other beggar waits in anticipation. That's life apparently; some get, some don't. We can't be generous to everyone. Yet the masterly figure is also carrying the scales of justice, symbolizing that he has the power to decide who should receive and who shouldn't. Meanwhile, he also gains approval for his generosity. Could this be an unconscious means of wielding power?

Whenever you draw this card in a "you now" position, consider whether your current kindness (in whatever form it takes) or act of giving is motivated by a need for power. Also question whether you are currently at the receiving end or the giving end of the equation. Are you gaining from someone's gifts, are you submitting to their will, are you taking what is due to you or not getting enough of what you want? Are they buying your love? Who is actually wielding the power?

The Six of Pentacles is a highly ambiguous card; therefore you must look at the other cards in the layout to determine which side of this particular "coin" you are on. The whole feel of the Six of Pentacles is very paradoxical. Up is down and black is white. Giving and receiving are one and the same thing, love and hate are not mutually exclusive. And, similarly, gain can be loss, gifts can be unwelcome, those who play victim or martyr can be omnipotent via their weakness.

This card in any layout suggests that you should dig a little deeper into your current motives, desires and apparent needs. We all want to profit, to gain, to achieve and advance.

This card indicates that it is time to lift the veil of illusion we have cast round these qualities and see that in those very gains there is also much of ourselves we lose. Similarly, in our losses there is very much to gain. In the "blockage" position, this card can mean any of the issues above.

Seven of Pentacles

KEY WORDS
Evaluation, fruits of labor, assessment

KEY PHRASES
- *Where or what next?*
- *Checking one's progress*
- *Evaluating where you are*
- *Making sure you are on target*
- *Prepared for a new strategy*
- *Ready to make your next move*
- *Seeing results for effort*
- *Having a break from hard work*

Interpretation

Well, this gardener has done well so far. The work he has put into making his garden grow has paid off and he's feeling a little more confident about his abilities. He has a harvest. But what next?

The Seven of Pentacles in a "you now" position indicates that it is time to take a reality-check on your progress. Think about how you have performed. What have you achieved so far and how can you enjoy the fruits of your labor? Maybe you've been so engrossed in your work or focus that you've forgotten to take stock of the results so far. But now it is assessment time.

Take a break and consider whether you actually need to invest more time and effort into your toils. Take a step back, rethink, create a new strategy or move off in a totally different direction. We sometime hang on to our current creation for fear of having to find a new one. Like painting a masterpiece or a sculpture, we need to know when to put down our tools and stop, otherwise we could make it a total disaster. We fear completion because it implies yet another new departure when we are quite happy going along the way we know and love. It is easier to stick with the familiar.

This card also indicates that you might be at a crossroads. It is important to evaluate where you are going and whether it is the right road for you now. It may have been comfortable and satisfying in the past, but now it is time to open yourself to the possibility of change. Any harvest means you've got to start again, sow more seeds, dig the earth and work hard on other aspects of your life. As a "blockage" card, persevere with your projects and don't sit around twiddling your thumbs. Act.

Eight of Pentacles

KEY WORDS

*Proficiency, diligence,
discipline, knowledge*

KEY PHRASES

- *Dedicated to the job*
- *Patient production*
- *Perseverance paying off*
- *Painstaking attention
  to detail*
- *Repetitive or boring
  situation*
- *Training for a new skill*
- *Widening your
  knowledge*

Interpretation

We work, we get down to the nitty-gritty, we pay attention to detail. Then sometimes we don't. When this card appears in a layout, it signifies that now is the time to get on with it. Concentrate all your energy on getting the job done, whatever it is. It may not necessarily be a practical job like the man chiselling away at his coins, but attend to your relationship, check the facts, read between the lines and give all your time to the task at hand. This card implies that you must persevere at all costs and the more you give out, the more you put into your work, belief, relationship or problem, the more successful will be the outcome.

Another interpretation of the Eight of Pentacles is that you have reached a level of proficiency where things have become a little too easy. You feel on top of it, but with that sense of achievement you need something else to get your teeth into—a new project, a new relationship. The Eight of Pentacles suggests that repetition and daily routines need to change so that you can shift into another gear. Time to add variety to your life in some way so you don't get bogged down in the same old thing.

In a "future outcome" position, it will soon be time to widen your perspective on the world. Take up a new skill, learn new techniques, make an effort to improve your knowledge. When in a "blockage" position, this card indicates that you are putting too much focus on your professional work at the cost of your relationship or personal development. Repairs and renewals are needed in the self-awareness department.

Nine of Pentacles

KEY WORDS

Accomplishment, refinement, independence, self-reliance

KEY PHRASES

- *Being resourceful*
- *Knowing you are in control of the situation*
- *Financial or material security*
- *Enjoying the finer pleasures of life*
- *An inner sense of security*
- *Acting on your own*
- *Self-discipline*

Interpretation

The Nine of Pentacles signifies that a mission has been accomplished. You are ready to enjoy yourself, indulge in your success and know that your way is the right way. As a result of your recent efforts in work or in your love life you have a greater sense of self-reliance and independence.

This graceful Pentacles lady feels secure in herself, she has a hooded falcon on her hand, representing our ability to control our feelings and demonstrate that we are not ruled by our unconscious doubts and fears. Falcons can be trained to hunt, to fly away, but always to come back to their perch. Likewise, you are free to do as you please, as long as you are down-to-earth and take responsibility for your actions.

This card also indicates that your most important duty right now is to yourself. Questions that need to be raised when you draw this card are: How free are you? Do you welcome independence? Have you acknowledged your accomplishments? Do you fear being self-reliant or believe you have nothing to show for your efforts?

If the Nine of Pentacles is in a "blockage" position, you may be literally so confident, self-assured and blasé that you are unable to let anyone get close to you. Or you believe you have now done everything you have intended, so what is there left to achieve?

This card can also represent sexual satisfaction, the indulgence of all the senses and a time for enjoyment in your intimate relationships.

Ten of Pentacles

KEY WORDS

The good life, wealth, convention, security, traditional values

KEY PHRASES

- *Sticking to the rules*
- *Wanting permanence and continuity*
- *Enjoying a happy family life*
- *Being secure materially*
- *Seeking affluence*
- *Emotional or spiritual prosperity*
- *Worldly success*

Interpretation

Although this card is traditionally associated with material affluence and family security, it is a slightly complex card. All these words—financial security, wealth, affluence and convention—are describing our most outward desires in the world. If we have lots of money, we believe our image is one of success. If we have a stable family life, then we are "good" people. If we follow the rules of convention, then we are not a threat to others. You get the picture.

When you draw this card you may well be going through a successful or prosperous phase; alternatively, you might long for greater wealth or are happy to stick to the rules knowing that conventional methods will get you places. The radical and the unpredictable are not welcome in the corridors of bureaucratic power.

There is nothing wrong with wanting more, as long as we are aware of the underlying motivation for that desire. There is nothing wrong with living a solid, stable family life, if you know what it truly means to you.

As a blockage card, this card often indicates that you are actually using the trappings of wealth, convention or family security for the wrong reasons, and that inside you are vulnerable, that change is uncomfortable, that lots of money or a successful career mean you won't feel so needy. We all need a certain amount of constancy in life, depending on our individual makeup. But the only certainty in life is that it does keep changing.

This card reminds you that long-lasting security is a very human need, and it can, of course, augur great enterprise, financial reward and the requisite number of children, but how long is a piece of string? The "they lived happily after" symbolism of this card is another of those very paradoxical symbols that keep cropping up in the tarot. Recognize your traditional values, follow the conventional pathway if that is your kind of trip, but don't fool yourself either.

Page of Pentacles

KEY WORDS

Practical approach, realistic aims, concentrated effort, focus and progress, new projects

KEY PHRASES

- *Setting the wheels in motion*
- *Looking for a window of opportunity*
- *Know your limitations*
- *Wanting to be prosperous*
- *Financial messenger*
- *Diligent worker*

Interpretation

The Page of Pentacles signifies that it is time to get practical or to progress with realistic aims and get involved in a new project. It is not so much simply looking at what you've achieved so far, but looking at the future to see what more you can accomplish. There is a window of opportunity out there, but you have got to look out for it. Whether it is literally a new career or enterprise, or a chance for greater clarity within a relationship, this card has a "let's get on with the job" feel about it.

The Page can also represent someone you know; a reliable worker, an organized friend, someone who knows how to turn vision into reality. This person may have something useful to tell you, or they may simply symbolize a part of yourself that you haven't yet expressed or acknowledged.

Ask yourself if you know your limitations; can you go further; how practical are you when it comes to working to have an effect on someone or something? Can you identify with planning and progress, focus and results? Or do you prevaricate and "put off until tomorrow what you could do today"?

These issues will arise with the Page of Pentacles in any spread, but make use of his positive influence to enjoy the spirit of commitment to a cause, or simply diligent planning. He can also appear in your life as reliable team player, a financial whiz-kid, a friend who has grounded ideas. If this appears as a "blockage" card, you are terribly self-focused; however, your goals and practical interests are taking top priority so that you are ignoring or are insensitive to the needs of others.

Knight of Pentacles

KEY WORDS

Hardworking, responsible, persistent, realistic

KEY PHRASES

- *A traditionalist*
- *Determined or dogmatic*
- *Realistic or gloomy*
- *Dedicated or inflexible*
- *Gets the task done*
- *Cautious or afraid to take a chance*
- *Effort without passion*
- *Faithfulness*
- *Someone slow to involve themselves in love*

Interpretation

When you draw this card, make sure you can relate to both extremes of energy that the Knight represents. Decide which is relevant to you now, and be honest enough to accept that, if you currently believe you are hard-working and persistent, you also might be expressing one of the Knight's negative qualities—being unadventurous or reluctant to do something new or different.

The Knight of Pentacles represents your ability to knuckle down and get on with the job, but also to avoid emotional involvement in that work. And that "work" includes anything from organizing your finances to being creative with a relationship. When we don't invest our feelings or passion into our efforts, we are cut off from the source of our individual conviction. This card reminds you that it is time to awaken those dormant, lost or missing passions, principles or beliefs if you want to improve your life.

The Knight of Pentacles in a "you now" position suggests that you are forthright and thorough, and willing to put time and effort into a project, but you would rather stay emotionally detached. If you have a relationship issue, this card suggests you are wary of getting involved too soon, perhaps denying your true feelings.

In a "blockage" position, the Knight of Pentacles signifies that you are either too stodgy or pessimistic, and that you need to lighten up a bit to clarify the situation or issue in mind. In any "future outcome" position, this Knight reminds you that caution, prudence and a thorough dose of realism are going to be invaluable, but take care you don't miss opportunities because you fear change. Embrace potentials instead of squashing them and you'll create your own success.

Queen of Pentacles

KEY WORDS

Dependable, nurturing, warmhearted, sensuous, generous, earth-mother

KEY PHRASES

- *Take a realistic view of life*
- *Matter-of-fact attitude*
- *Reliable and loyal*
- *Feeling secure and home-loving*
- *Genuine desire to help other people*
- *Lover of animals and children*
- *Creative and resourceful*

Interpretation

The Queen of Pentacles takes us further into the realm of our sense of security and connectedness to the world. She is there for everyone, always available, reliable, home-loving, willing to do anything for her clan and all without any fuss. She is the kind of person you admire, envy or even hate.

Think about what this archetypal earth-mother makes you feel. Do you identify with her at all? Do you admire her loyalty, her warm heart and unpretentious lifestyle? Do you envy her natural, sensible approach to any problem, or do you loathe the way she welcomes anyone into her cozy lair? Or are you totally immune to feeling anything?

Whatever your reaction, remember that the Queen of Pentacles represents a part of you. The energy she symbolizes may come into your life via someone else—perhaps a new face in the social crowd, a family member, a new partner (male or female, the Queen of Pentacles indicates the feminine qualities of earthiness and nurturing).

Whoever the Queen represents, she also points a finger at you, and says, "look within, find your nurturing side." Do you look after yourself? Do you care about someone else? Are you able to remain a dependable friend or lover, or will you give away their secrets? Have you developed your creative talents or given up on them? If the Queen appears in a "blockage" position, you are nurturing others at the expense of your own emotional or spiritual needs.

King of Pentacles

KEY WORDS

Reliable, savvy, materialistic, enterprising, supportive

KEY PHRASES

- *Charismatic character*
- *Business leader*
- *Financial adviser*
- *Practical and stabilizing*
- *Resolute and unshakeable*
- *The "Midas touch"*
- *Competent, no-nonsense approach*
- *Responsible attitude*

Interpretation

This is one happy king. He has made a success of something, reached the top, has no hang-ups or complexes and has that uncanny ability to be one step ahead of the game. The King of Pentacles represents an enterprising and reliable personality. Someone who knows what's best for themselves and others, knows how to wheel and deal, has an instinct for how things work, and is as reliable as the rock of Gibraltar. In fact, this is one King we'd all like to know. He may already be in your life, perhaps someone you know or work with who will inspire some of these qualities in you.

The King of Pentacles sometimes indicates that you are in a successful period of your life, and must be resolved to carry on. Enjoy what you are doing and don't feel guilty for your achievements. Alternatively, this energy may be lacking in your life, and now needs to be expressed.

As a "blockage" card, you may be so obsessed with your business or financial world that your relationships are suffering. Or someone else might be forcing you to take on more than you can handle. As a "future outcome" card, the King of Pentacles says, "reap the rewards of your efforts, make that commitment in love (or make love in a pile of money!), go for the gold, climb to the top of your profession." With this card you will have the energy, confidence and charisma to handle any situation.

Everyday
spreads

How to use the everyday spreads

The spreads in this section are designed to give you quick and easy access to reading the tarot. Whether a beginner or an experienced reader, these everyday spreads are useful for resolving simple issues or for self-awareness on a daily basis. The layout patterns used can be adapted, as can the key word phrases for each card position.

These easy spreads are great for developing your own personal interpretations of the cards rather than always projecting the same meaning onto them. Rather like reading the same paragraph over and over again, you can become bored with what you are reading if you don't move on to the next page. You can also use them as simple "past," "present" and "future" spreads or relate them to specific issues.

The art of interpreting the spreads is always to remember they are a reflection of you at the moment you choose to lay out the cards. If you can be objective, so much the better; so try to create a story around the cards first. Tell your story out loud to force yourself to structure what is going on in your head. Remember that if you are looking for an answer, the solution may not necessarily be found in any individual card, but in the total layout itself.

The focus of these everyday spreads will enable you to get to know more about the cards individually before you start to use more complicated spreads. They will help you to understand that you are looking in a mirror and determine which cards bring up issues for you. When you are only working with a few cards in a layout, one card is more likely to "speak" to you. You suddenly have a flash and *know* what it means. Then again, you might hate another card, or fear its implications. Ask yourself why the cards are pushing your psychological buttons. In these daily readings you can find out a lot more about yourself than you imagine and have fun getting to know the cards, too.

With practice you will become more in tune with the cards.

Before you begin

There are no rules about laying out spreads or interpreting them, but the following guidelines provide a framework and structure from which to work. Structure and substance is the world of the suit of Pentacles, interpretation is a combination of Swords and Wands, and Cups represent our response to that interpretation.

Step-by-step guide

1 Make sure you are in a quiet, comfortable environment. This will allow you to focus and let your intuition flow. Create enough space to lay out the cards on the floor or on an empty table.

2 Light candles and incense or play soft music to soften your mood and allow you to focus.

3 Perform your favorite ritual.

4 Keep a tarot journal near you for making notes or comments.

5 Write down your question or issue before you begin.

It is important to make notes in your journal when you start using the tarot.

Important

Throughout the spreads there are example readings to give you guidance. Also remember that not all the spreads have "you now," "blockage" or "future outcome" positions that are referred to in the Interpretation segment for each individual card. If you choose a layout that doesn't include these specific positions, interpret the card with its definitive meanings.

6 Shuffle the cards in one of the recommended ways (see pages 54–55) and cut three times.

7 As you shuffle, keep focusing on your question if you have one.

8 One by one, choose the relevant number of cards for the layout you have chosen. Choosing the card is the moment when you and the tarot cards merge. If you have a question or issue, focus on the subject or repeat the question to yourself while you draw each card.

9 Lay each card down one at a time, *face-down,* in the order and position that are shown in the spread diagram.

10 When all the cards have been laid out, turn them face up one at a time and put them the right way up if any are reversed.

11 Get to know each of the cards, and check the interpretations in this book with your own feelings and intuition. Really decide what each card means for you before you move on to the next. When you are more experienced you will find you can combine cards and even read the whole layout as one.

12 Follow the key word text for each spread as well as the accompanying advice.

Daily Practice

These are two good ways to get to know the cards on a daily basis. Apart from drawing just one card for the day to see what occurs, these two spreads require your input and will allow you to have direct experience of the cards' meanings via self-questioning.

Card for the day spread

1 Card for the day (the important aspects of the day ahead)
2 Attend to this (personal issues that will require attention)
3 What to look out for (feelings, desires or reactions that could arise)

Example reading

1 Strength A day when you will take responsibility for your actions; emotional strength combined with compassion is the key to successful relationships and dealings. Interactive question: how in touch are you with your emotional nature?

2 Eight of Pentacles Be diligent, pay attention to details and dedicate yourself to a task. Does this feel threatening or satisfying?

3 Seven of Cups Wishful thinking or kidding yourself that you know all the answers. People who daydream or are sloppy—do they annoy you or do you go with their flow?

Mood of your day spread

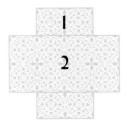

1 The mood of your day
2 Interferences
3 Positive results

Example reading

1 Four of Wands Your mood is exuberant, free and easy. Do you resist or welcome those feelings?

2 The Emperor Interferences to your mood might be authority figures, your own need to take control. Can you let go of all responsibilities

1   2   3

for a day and enjoy yourself? Are others stopping you from doing what you want?

3 King of Swords A day when you can also cut through the confusion and analyze the situation. How rational are you?

My greatest strength and my greatest weakness

You can either use these two spreads individually or lay them out side-by-side and thread the interpretations together. Notice how your current strength and current weakness may be two sides of the same coin. How are these qualities operating in your life?

My greatest strength spread

1 My current strength
2 How I can utilize it
3 The road it will lead to
4 What strength I need to develop

Example reading

1 **Page of Pentacles** Realistic attitude. How well acquainted am I with that?
2 **Three of Swords** Deal with my wounds. Accept that I have them.
3 **Wheel of Fortune** A crossroads, a turning point. Think about how well or not I handle change.
4 **Hanged Man** Going with the flow. Living for the moment.

My greatest weakness spread

1 My current weakness
2 What will help me overcome it
3 New direction

Example reading

1 Seven of Wands Refusing to budge or change my viewpoint on principle.
2 The Star An optimistic outlook on life, fresh ideals, belief in my dreams.
3 Ace of Swords Time to be honest with myself and cut through outdated illusions.

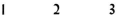

1   2   3

My priorities right now

These two layouts deal with issues that must be attended to. The first layout uses a five-card layout with the first card being the priority, followed by related cards that reveal any problems surrounding that priority and how to deal with it to progress. Other priorities usually concern your love life, career and self-development, but you can change the categories if you like.

Example reading

1 Six of Cups My main priority right now is to be generous or kind or to have good intentions for myself and others.

2 The Devil I'm thinking negatively, obsessed with materialism.

3 Two of Pentacles Begin to juggle with ideas, be more adaptable.

4 Queen of Swords My hidden motives for how I act.

5 Nine of Cups I should get the results I'm hoping for.

3

1

2

5

4

My main priority spread

1 Main priority
2 What is blocking me
3 Things I can change
4 Things I must accept
5 How things will progress

1   2   3   4   5

Other priorities spread

1 Love
2 Career
3 Self-improvement

Example reading

1 **The Hermit** I need to think more seriously about what kind of love is right for me.

2 **Three of Wands** It is also time to try something new or different.

3 **Ten of Pentacles** Financial security is important to my well-being right now.

1   2   3

The secret me

These two spreads reveal your current secrets. You can do this spread quite often, as our secret moods, feelings and desires change all the time. Our fear of accepting that feelings change prevents us from moving on.

Secret me spread 1

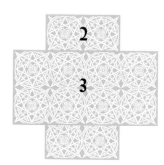

1 My secret desire
2 What motivates me
3 What puts me down
4 What I can accomplish

Example reading

1 **The Chariot** I really want to be in control of my life.

2 **Eight of Pentacles** Working hard and dedicating myself to a task.

3 **Eight of Wands** I get worried when things move too quickly or are up in the air.

4 **The Star** It is time to share my ideas and be inspired into action.

Secret me spread 2

1 My secret love
2 My secret hate
3 My secret test

Example reading
1 The Tower My secret love is an electrifying relationship or is creating chaos around me.
2 Six of Wands My secret hate is toward people who strut their stuff.
3 The Magician My secret test is to acknowledge my motivations for both of the above.

1   **2**   **3**

Favorite and least favorite cards

This spread is a little different from the others because first you must consciously choose two cards—your current favorite and your current least favorite—from the pack. Take your time to look through the cards and, if several seem to leap out at you at once, remove them from the pack and narrow them down to one each. You may find that favorites and least favorites change quite frequently, depending on your situation.

Step-by-step guide

1 Lay out the first two cards in the positions shown on page 269, then shuffle the rest of the pack as normal. Choose one card at random and lay it face down in position 3.

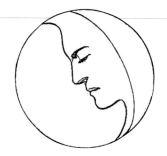

2 First look up the interpretations for your favorite and least favorite cards. Think about what each card means for you right now. Why do you like one and loathe the other?

3 Is the card you loathe particularly significant; are you blocking out these emotions or archetypal energies or do you project them onto others?

4 Is the card you like projected onto a lover, an ideal or a long-term ambition? Are you actually living out this quality or just daydreaming about it?

5 Finally, turn over your third card and discover what you need to learn right now about these two cards.

Favorite and least favorite spread

1

2

3

1 Favorite card
2 Least favorite card
3 What you need to learn

Example reading

1 Queen of Pentacles My favorite card is how I would like to be, reliable and loyal.

2 The Moon The Moon represents my inability to trust others.

3 Strength I need to learn to be more self-aware and to take responsibility for my actions, to learn to trust others and myself.

1   2   3

Past issue, present obstacle, future outlook

This layout uses the past, present and future to give you a sense of the threads of life which are all interwoven in time. We always want to know what the future holds because it gives us a sense of control over our lives. But it is also important to know what was in the past, because, although the past is another country, it is part of our present. We think about the past all the time, probably as much as we do the future. Unravel the threads of the past and you can see how to deal with the future and make it your own.

Past, present, future spread

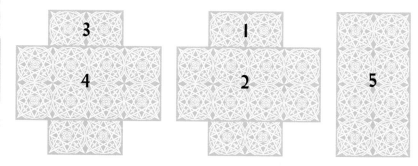

1 You now
2 Present obstacle
3 Past issue still unresolved
4 Past obstacle
5 The way ahead

Example reading

1 The High Priestess I want to reveal my
feelings to someone.

2 King of Swords But I feel vulnerable
about opening up for fear of the risk of
criticism or being put down.

3 Two of Cups I've always taken things
too personally and get hurt and defensive
too easily.

4 Two of Pentacles I was always trying to juggle with too
many things and never focused on who I am and what I want.

5 Nine of Pentacles Being more emotionally independent; then I won't fear
telling someone how I really feel.

1   2   3   4   5

All change

Another "future/past-oriented" spread, but this time you focus on what you can let go of from the past to enable you to move on. This spread is very helpful if you are clinging to the past, unable to detach yourself from a relationship wound or feelings of rejection. Or simply just to say "good-bye" to the old you and welcome the new.

What I need to resolve spread

1 What no longer matters
2 What has been fulfilled
3 What will carry me forward
4 The change I must embrace

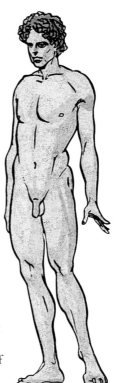

Example reading

1 The Lovers What no longer matters is a love affair that is finished.

2 Five of Swords What has been fulfilled is that I've accepted my limitations.

3 The Sun What will carry me forward is knowing that there is more happiness to come.

4 Queen of Cups The change I must embrace is that of opening up to others and being more compassionate.

1   2   3   4

Who I am now and where I'm going

This spread invites you to explore yourself a little more thoroughly than the others, using a seven-card layout.

Who and where spread

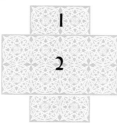

1 This is who I am now
2 This is what I don't know about myself
3 This is what I need to relinquish
4 This is what I need to develop
5 What I'd love to become
6 My current quest
7 Where it will lead

| 1 | 2 | 3 | 4 | 5 | 6 | 7 |

Example reading

1 Eight of Pentacles I am currently hard-working and self-focused.

2 Judgement What I don't know about myself is that I can drop old values and find new ones. I can make choices and take responsibility for my actions.

3 Page of Cups What I need to relinquish is always being too eager to please everyone else.

4 King of Swords What I need to develop is a more discerning outlook.

5 The Hermit What I'd love to become is more reflective and more in tune with myself.

6 Ace of Wands My current quest is to believe in myself and follow up on my visions and ideals.

7 Three of Pentacles This will lead to me making new contacts, working as part of a team and proving I can make a go of it.

Relationship spreads

How to use the relationship spreads

We all know how complex relationships can be and, whether we're just falling in love and infatuated by the mystery of it all, or feeling wounded, betrayed or bored with a current relationship, there are times when we need to turn to the tarot to give us an objective look at what's going on. Whatever reason you have for consulting the tarot, it is a good one. And the tarot will mirror your relationships just as it mirrors you.

This section includes card spreads that can be used either by you alone or with your partner or lover. When opting to do these spreads alone, take a very careful and honest look at the cards that fall into the territory of the "other," since you will be interpreting your partner's cards on their behalf. Interpreting cards for an absent party is always fraught with projection about what you "want" your lover to feel, think or do. But, if you can be totally honest and

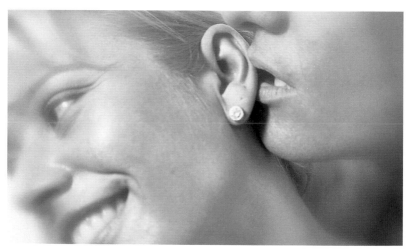

If you combine your and your partner's birthdays you will get a unique card.

objective, then using these relationship spreads can give some remarkable insights into your relationship.

Reading spreads with a partner

When reading with a partner, make sure you agree between you who will be partner A or B. As you will see in some of the spread diagrams, there are distinct positions for partner A and B cards.

Sit face-to-face on the floor and take turns shuffling the cards so that both of you have handled the cards. To choose or draw cards, form a long line of the shuffled cards face-down between you so that you can each choose a card in turn. Lay them down one at a time in succession. If you do a spread that has one card to represent the relationship itself (in other words, the combined energy of you both), decide beforehand who will choose that particular card.

The relationship card

Using your combined birthdays, you can also work out your current relationship Major Arcana card. This shows the challenges, tendencies and interplay between you and your partner. If it comes up in a reading it will reinforce the underlying dynamic of that position. The Fool is 0 but for this process you'll have to make it 22—no addition can become 0.

The relationship card is determined by adding both of your birthdays together, and then adding the digits together to arrive at a number below 22. For example:

May 26, 1952 and March 28, 1950
26 + 5 + 1952 + 28 + 3 + 1950 = 3964
3 + 9 + 6 + 4 = 22

The Fool is given the number 22 so this is the relationship Major Arcana card.

The relationship right now

This spread (done either solo or as a duo) can help you understand your relationship at any point in time, identify its plus and minus points and guide you and your partner through the maze of emotions. Love's energy is never static and this spread can show you how and where it is moving right now.

Slightly different from the others because you are mirroring a relationship, not yourself, this spread reveals the dynamics and interplay between you. The cards represent the mechanics of the relationship rather than you or your partner. Treat the relationship as a third party and yourselves as onlookers.

Note: For this spread, use the Major Arcana cards only for an in-depth interpretation.

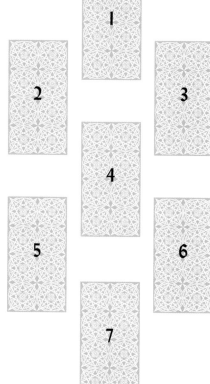

The relationship and its qualities

1 Its energy
2 Its communication
3 Its strength
4 Its weakness
5 Its reality
6 Its passion
7 Its key to the future

1   2   3   4   5   6   7

Example reading

1 Temperance The relationship is harmonious and balanced.

2 The Star There is an idealistic but progressive dialogue going on in this relationship.

3 The Sun Creativity and playfulness are the key to its success.

4 The Chariot There seems to be an underlying power play going on. Who can outwit whom?

5 The High Priestess There is an air of mystery surrounding this relationship to the outsider.

6 The World Adventurous and extrovert.

7 The Lovers Mutual decisions and honesty will keep this relationship very much alive.

The love test

This spread (done solo) can be used whether you are in a new or long-term relationship or still single. It gives you the chance to explore what love means to you or if you want a relationship to work, and how to move forward successfully or find the right partner.

The love goal spread
1 My love goal
2 What I have to offer
3 What I lack
4 What I don't want in a partner
5 What I do want in a partner
6 The heart of the matter
7 What I can do to make this work

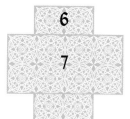

Example reading

1 The Hermit My goal is to discover my inner truth through a close love relationship.

2 Four of Wands I can offer my spontaneity and joie de vivre.

3 Ten of Cups I lack a sense of family or belonging.

4 Seven of Swords I don't want deceptive behavior in a partner.

5 Page of Wands I want creativity and an adventurous spirit in a partner.

6 The Hanged Man I must accept who I am and not try to sacrifice my needs for the sake of being loved.

7 The Magician To make it work, I can be more self-aware, to acknowledge my motivations and intentions.

| 1 | 2 | 3 | 4 | 5 | 6 | 7 |

How you see each other

Use this spread on your own or with a partner to reveal the truth of how you each view the other and the relationship. If you do this alone, remember not to project your hopes, fears or wishes onto your partner. Sometimes it can be helpful to have an objective friend interpret the cards for you.

Note: Decide beforehand who is A and who is B.

Seeing each other spread

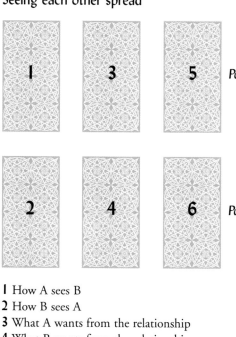

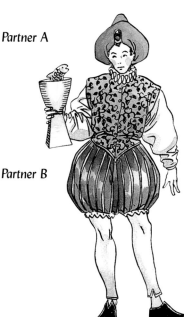

Partner A

Partner B

1 How A sees B
2 How B sees A
3 What A wants from the relationship
4 What B wants from the relationship
5 Where A believes this relationship is going
6 Where B believes this relationship is going

I 2 3 4 5 6

Example reading

I Queen of Wands A sees B as energetic, extrovert and enthusiastic.

2 Judgement B sees A as decisive, honest, a good judge of the situation.

3 Page of Cups A wants companionship, a good social life and to feel bonded.

4 Six of Swords B wants to move on from past emotional baggage and make a fresh start.

5 Four of Pentacles A believes the relationship is going to stagnate unless they make an effort to move on.

6 The Hierophant B believes the relationship is going along as normal, a truly conventional relationship.

Obviously, A and B need to discuss the future, as A is worried about the relationship becoming boring and routine, and B doesn't see that as an issue.

These kinds of discrepancies often arise when you try these relationship spreads, but it can create an opening for creative dialogue and mutual understanding of the deeper issues at stake.

Where do we go from here?

Like the previous spread, this can be done solo or together, and helps you look at the state of your relationship and where it might be going.

Where are we going spread

1 Where we are now
2 What is causing us a problem
3 What we have forgotten to respect
4 What we need to express
5 Our options
6 Where we will go from here

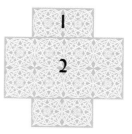

| I | 2 | 3 | 4 | 5 | 6 |

Example reading

1 Strength At the moment we are giving each other lots of space and accepting each other's faults.

2 Temperance Too much cooperation, always willing to find the middle ground could be causing problems right now. Could this be a little dull and unstimulating?

3 Six of Cups We have forgotten how to play.

4 Seven of Cups We need to express our dreams, our need to be a little self-indulgent and laid-back about life.

5 The Fool Our options are to expand our horizons, network, do something spontaneous, be more carefree.

6 Ace of Cups From here we could fall in love again, get closer to each other. Let romance blossom.

As you can see, all may be well on the surface, harmony abounds and you are giving each other space. What more could you want? But there is always a "problem" or "lack" or "need" in any relationship. This spread allows you to go down that road and see how to move on and create an animated relationship rather than a static one.

Sexual chemistry lesson

This is fun to do either on your own or with your partner. If you do this as a duo, make it clear before you start who is going to be "you" and "me." But please note that the expressions "I make you feel" and "you make me feel" are very judgmental. We all say "you make me feel fantastic, great, young etc." In fact, what we're saying is that there is something about you that triggers off the "fantastic," "young" or whatever side of my personality. Note: for this spread use only the court cards, Aces and the Major Arcana.

Sexual chemistry spread

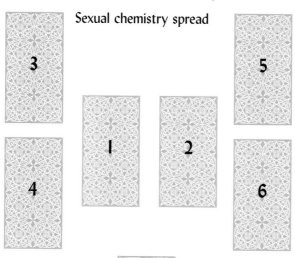

1 My sexual style right now is . . .
2 Your sexual style right now is . . .
3 I'm passionate about you because . . .
4 You are passionate about me because . . .
5 You make me feel . . .
6 I make you feel . . .
7 Our sexual alchemy is . . .

| 1 | 2 | 3 | 4 | 5 | 6 | 7 |

Example spread

1 Queen of Swords My sexual style is exciting, bold.

2 Knight of Swords Your sexual style is challenging, expressive.

3 Queen of Pentacles I'm passionate about you right now because you represent beauty and truth.

4 The Emperor You are passionate about me right now because I represent sexual power.

5 Ace of Wands You make me feel rushed, as if I'm taking things too fast.

6 King of Swords I make you feel articulate, sure of your sexuality.

7 Knight of Wands Our sexual alchemy is daring and reckless.

You and me

This spread, like the previous spreads, can be done solo or as a duo. Please note that this spread is slightly different from the others because the seventh card is not drawn randomly like the other six. It is the sum total of all the cards you have drawn so far. In other words, it represents the combined energies of you both. To find this card, simply add up the numerical value of the other six cards once you have drawn them.

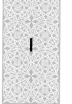

Feelings, desires and regrets spread

1 My feelings are . . .
2 My desires are . . .
3 My regrets are . . .
4 Your feelings are . . .
5 Your desires are . . .
6 Your regrets are . . .
7 Our future is . . .

Example reading

1 Queen of Wands My feelings are dramatic.

2 The Lovers My desires are passionate.

3 Five of Swords My regrets are that I've been too self-interested.

4 The Moon Your feelings are bewildered.

5 Justice Your desires are about finding honesty and truth.

6 Ten of Swords Your regrets are that you've always played the martyr.

7 The Chariot Our future is to confront the truth and create our own unique pathway.

| 1 | 2 | 3 | 4 | 5 | 6 | 7 |

Obviously, when you interpret the cards explore more fully the interpretations rather than just using one word; this simply gives you the basis for each card interpretation.

To determine your seventh card, add up the numerical value of each card; for example, the Lovers is 6, the Ten of Swords is 10, and give a numerical value of 1 for a King, 2 for a Queen, 3 for a Knight and 4 for a Page. Add up the numbers and arrive at a number between 1 and 22 (the Fool is 0, but for this process you'll have to make it 22—no addition can become 0). Then check which Major Arcana card is your special future card.

Hurt feelings

This solo spread is called "ouch" because it can hurt. The point is to understand a little more deeply what it is about your partner and yourself that sparks off hurt feelings at any given moment. These hurt feelings cause your defense mechanisms to slip sharply into gear. But by working with this insight you can see yourself with clarity, and see where the relationship is going.

Love, hurt and defend spread

1 How I love you
2 How I hurt you
3 How I defend myself
4 How you love me
5 How you hurt me
6 How you defend yourself
7 Who am I right now?
8 Who are you right now?
9 Where are we going?

Example reading

1 Knight of Swords I love you frankly and unequivocally.

2 Ten of Cups But I hurt you by appearing to be more tied to my family or family values than to you.

3 Seven of Wands I defend myself by refusing to see any other viewpoint.

4 Nine of Swords You love me in a very anxious, guilty sort of way.

5 The Lovers Yes and so you hurt me by flirting with others.

6 Three of Cups You defend yourself by saying everyone's your friend and you don't believe in exclusive relationships.

7 Wheel of Fortune Right now I'm at a turning point.

8 The Tower Right now you are going to have a blow to your ego.

9 The Ace of Swords We are going to have to face the truth and accept responsibility for our actions and words.

1 2 3 4 5

6 7 8 9

Partnership truth spread

This spread, done either by yourself or with your partner, takes you a few steps deeper than all the other relationship layouts. If you are willing to work through this one with your partner in complete honesty and objectivity, it can be extremely rewarding and lead to greater mutual understanding.

Truth spread

Partner A

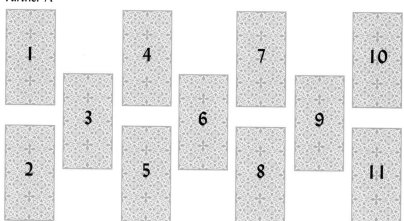

Partner B

1 Me now
2 You now
3 Our joint goal/aspiration
4 Do I really want this?
5 Do you really want this?
6 Our current illusion

7 How I can help fix it
8 How you can help fix it
9 Our hidden/unspoken agenda
10 What I'm projecting onto you
11 What you are projecting onto me

Example reading

This reading doesn't do this spread real justice, because it is the interpretation you make in relation to each statement or question that is crucial.

1 King of Swords I am currently articulate and analytical.

2 Eight of Pentacles You are dedicated to current projects.

3 Four of Swords Our current joint goal is to take life easy.

4 Four of Cups Yes, I really want this. I need to hold back a little.

5 The Devil I'm not so sure, I'm really attached to materialism, can't imagine giving it all up for an alternative lifestyle.

6 The Fool Our current illusion is pursuing a pipe dream which is unrealistic.

7 Two of Cups I can help to fix it by connecting better to you.

8 Justice You can help to fix it by taking more responsibility for choices.

9 Three of Swords Our hidden unspoken agenda is that we both fear being hurt so we avoid the truth.

10 Ten of Cups I'm projecting family values onto you.

11 Knight of Wands You are projecting your exaggerated talents onto me.

Mirroring

Another revealing spread to do alone
or together; if you are totally honest it
will help you learn to respect each
other's individual perceptions of the
relationship. If you do this on your
own, do make sure you are totally
objective about partner B's answers.

Mirroring spread

1 What I am or think I am
2 What you are or think you are
3 This is what I feel
4 This is what you feel
5 This is what I think you feel
6 This is what you think I feel
7 This is what I want to happen
8 This is what you want to happen
9 This is the outcome

Partner A

Partner B

Example reading

1 Page of Wands I think I am creative and self-confident.

2 The Star You think you are inspirational and idealistic.

3 The Empress I feel vibrant and nurturing.

4 Five of Swords You feel people are out to get you.

5 Knight of Wands I think you feel sexy and seductive.

6 The Chariot You think I feel competitive and self-assured.

7 Eight of Cups I want to move on to better things.

8 Six of Wands You want to achieve success.

9 Queen of Swords The outcome is that we must get to the heart of the matter and sort it out.

Secrets

We often hide our feelings even from ourselves. This solo layout allows you to explore your true inner feelings for yourself and your partner.

Secrets spread

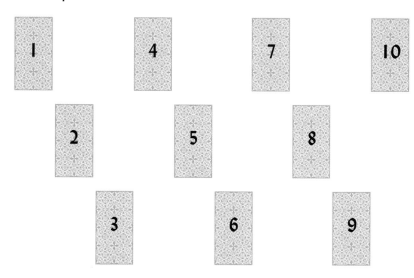

1 My secret desire for myself
2 My secret fear for myself
3 My secret weapon for myself
4 My secret feeling (for you)
5 My secret love (for you)

6 My secret hate (for you)
7 My secret fantasy (for us both)
8 My secret power
9 My secret vulnerability
10 My biggest secret

| 1 | 2 | 3 | 4 | 5 |

| 6 | 7 | 8 | 9 | 10 |

Example reading

1 The High Priestess My secret desire is to take this relationship slowly, to be a little more enigmatic and elusive.

2 Eight of Wands My secret fear is that it is all moving too fast.

3 Death My secret weapon is that I can accept the changes that must now take place.

4 Three of Cups My secret feelings for you are exuberant; I want to dance and sing and play forever.

5 The Moon My secret love for you is filled with fear; I'm not sure if you're deceiving me.

6 Temperance I secretly hate your sensible, compromising side.

7 Nine of Cups My secret fantasy is that we'll make love for ever.

8 Six of Wands My secret power is that I can strut my stuff.

9 Queen of Swords My secret vulnerability is that I repress my emotions.

10 The Lovers My biggest secret right now is that I want a long-term commitment.

Revelation spreads

How to use the revelation spreads

The following spreads give you further insight into your own personal world. They continue the themes you found in the everyday spreads but are more detailed and more focused on self-development than on simple "workouts." They reveal more about you and your inner world, what makes you tick, what you really want for yourself, and subsequently give you the opportunity to take responsibility for your own life choices and personal growth.

As with the everyday spreads and the relationships spreads, the art of interpreting is always to remember that they are a reflection of you at the moment you choose to lay the cards.

If you find it hard to combine the ideas or interpret the cards in relation to yourself or current issues, try to create a story around the cards, and say it out loud to force yourself to structure the ideas in your head. The solution may not necessarily be found in any individual card, but in the total layout itself.

By now you should know the best way to shuffle and choose random cards. Again, like the previous spreads, lay the cards out in the order shown in the diagram, face down. Turn any reversed card into the upright position and work slowly.

Knowledge of your inner world will bring you outer happiness.

Write down your thoughts and feelings after doing a spread.

Important

Throughout the spreads there are example readings to give you guidance, but we can't go into much detail due to limited space. Also remember not all the spreads have "you now," "blockage" or "future outcome" positions that are referred to regularly in each card's individual interpretation. If you choose a layout that doesn't include these specific positions, interpret the card's main meanings or develop the theme that surrounds the card to work it into your plot of the spread.

You can use the patterns of these spreads to develop your own layouts and specific question-related readings.

What am I doing with my life?

This is a life-affirming spread that gives you positive direction if you feel stuck or unsure of where to go from here. It enables you to see the past influences in relation to future intentions, and to move on accordingly.

5

3

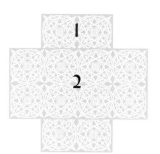

1

2

6

What am I doing spread

1 Me now
2 What I am afraid of
3 Past influence—beneficial
4 Past influence—negative
5 I promise myself this
6 This will be the result

4

Example reading

1 Five of Pentacles I am currently feeling rejected and left out in the cold.

2 The Tower I am afraid of sudden change or unexpected developments because I won't be in control of the situation.

3 King of Wands A recent beneficial influence on me was a charismatic person or a feeling that I could be more courageous and motivated.

4 Nine of Swords A recent negative influence was feeling guilty about wanting to be true to myself.

5 Six Pentacles But I promise myself that I'm going to make sure I know exactly where I am in all this. Am I giving away too much of myself? Am I taking too much or expecting too much from others? This is what I have to sort out.

6 The World The result will be that I experience a better sense of wholeness and can begin to realize my goals.

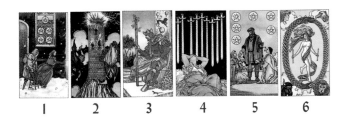

The problem, suggestion, and answer

Use this very simple three-card spread when you have
some kind of personal problem, but don't know what to
do next. You may have a very strong awareness of what
needs fixing: a broken relationship, a dead-end job, a
restless desire to travel or the fear of commitment. The
first card will focus on the root of the problem, what lies
behind the manifestation of the problem and the
second will help you resolve the situation. Problems
are rather like symptoms; you must look at the
underlying cause for the symptom and attempt to
remedy the hidden cause.

Problem, suggestion and answer spread

1 This is the root of my current problem
2 This is how to deal with it
3 The resolution

1   2   3

Example reading

Liz's problem is that she is bored with all her friends.

1 Five of Swords The root of my boredom lies in thinking only of myself, isolating myself and defining my interests too narrowly. I don't take time out to listen to others or give anyone a chance to get close to me.

2 Five of Cups The way to deal with it is to accept that things must change and I must let go of my past patterns of behavior, however "safe" they made me feel.

3 King of Cups My resolution is to be more tolerant and caring, open my eyes to others and learn new ideas. Maybe then I won't be so bored. Perhaps I need to learn that my boredom says more about me than about my friends.

Outer attitude, inner truth

This spread reveals your inner truth and the façade that is on show to the world. The latter may not necessarily be in accord with your deeper feelings or intentions. Why not? Sometimes we fear that if we do what we really want deep down inside, we won't be loved. So maybe it is time to be more honest about what you want and be prepared to stand up for yourself. The cards that cross the inner truth cards represent the source of resistance (whether from within you or from a third party), or those things that are contrary to your inner intentions.

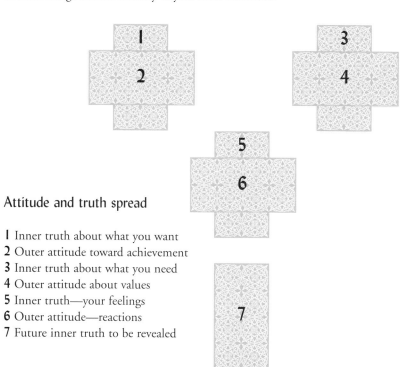

Attitude and truth spread

1 Inner truth about what you want
2 Outer attitude toward achievement
3 Inner truth about what you need
4 Outer attitude about values
5 Inner truth—your feelings
6 Outer attitude—reactions
7 Future inner truth to be revealed

Example reading

1 The Magician What you want deep down inside is to make an impact, to do something no one else has even dreamed of.

2 Knight of Cups But your outer attitude to achievement is unrealistic and often totally fanciful so no one really believes or trusts you.

3 Strength What you truly need is patience and self-determination.

4 Nine of Cups But you appear to value material gain over and above personal integrity.

5 Three of Swords Deep down you feel incredibly lonely, as if you are in emotional exile.

6 Three of Wands But you are good at covering this up either with your ability to set an example or with your leadership skills.

7 Seven of Swords The inner truth revealed is that you must face the facts and stop running away from the truth. Don't deceive yourself.

1 2 3 4 5 6 7

Current challenges, future outcomes

This spread allows you to explore the current challenges you may need to resolve in your life.

Challenges and outcomes spread

1 Personal challenge right now
2 Relationship challenge right now
3 What holds me back?
4 What motivates me?
5 Where will I get support?
6 What decision do I need to make based on the above?
7 The outcome

| 1 | 2 | 3 | 4 | 5 | 6 | 7 |

Example reading

1 Six of Cups My personal challenge is to stop being such a do-gooder or so nice for fear of rejection. Alternatively, my personal challenge is to be more appreciative of the simple pleasures of life. (Remember all cards have shades of meaning.)

2 Eight of Swords My relationship challenge is to stop feeling so restricted or victimized and to discover clarity and direction.

3 Ten of Cups What is stopping me from moving forward? Well, probably my belief that family values matter more than personal ones or that I'm supposed to be happy in a family setting. I have a sense of guilt around that.

4 Page of Wands What really motivates me is adventure and risk taking. I want some freedom.

5 Ace of Wands Where will I discover support? From original, enthusiastic people with spirit and confidence to back my own. (The Ace of Wands may not represent a person directly, but the theme of the Ace of Wands implies creativity, so, similarly, be creative with your tarot language.)

6 Death What decision do I need to make based on the above? To decide now is the time to close one door and open another; to accept that I have to make a big change in my life. To stop being someone I'm not. Personal freedom is my aim and my guilt around family and always playing the "blue-eyed boy/girl" is stopping me from being true to myself.

7 The High Priestess The outcome is that at last I can reveal all my hidden talents and express my individuality.

What I need to learn

We all have things to learn as we travel on the road of life. Sometimes the learning curve involved is really steep; sometimes it is barely a bump on the horizon. This spread focuses on the three main areas—love, life and career—to help you take the next step along the road. The three cards for each theme can be read individually or combined. The latter is a good exercise in seeing the whole answer in more than one card. Remember to interpret both the "positive" and "negative" aspects of each card; the positive qualities may be lacking or the negative qualities need to be transformed to positive ones.

Learning spread

1, 2, 3 What I need to learn about love
4, 5, 6 What I need to learn about life
7, 8, 9 What I need to learn about my vocation

Example reading

1, 2, 3 Queen of Swords, Ten of Wands, Justice In love, I need to learn to be upfront or honest about my feelings; to stop feeling it is my duty to make someone else happy; to stop taking the blame for everything that goes wrong. I need to learn to take responsibility for my choices.

4, 5, 6 Two of Cups, the Moon, the Hermit In life, I must learn that it is important to forgive and forget, and to accept others as equals. I must also learn to know the difference between my illusions and what I can actually achieve or do. I must now look deeper within myself for meaning and self-awareness.

7, 8, 9 The Devil, Eight of Cups, the Wheel of Fortune In my career, I need to focus less on material gain and stop doubting myself or my talents. Now is the time to move on, expand my outlook and take up the opportunity that is coming my way.

Letting go of the past

This spread is slightly different from the others because you must first choose a card that represents the thing, idea, person, complex, dynamic, feeling or whatever you want to leave behind. This makes you focus on the issue itself, and means that you have to work a little harder than if you simply drew a card at random to represent the "disposable" subject.

Look at the 22 Major Arcana separately and decide which one represents your issue. For example, if you want to forget an ex who continues to haunt you, you might choose the Lovers (you can't stop desiring them); the Emperor (a dominant, controlling partner); or the Devil (your partner was selfish, more interested in money and power than true love).

Next, shuffle all the cards and draw the other five cards as normal.

Letting go spread

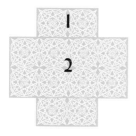

1 I want to let go of ...
2 What is stopping me?
3 How to move forward
4 Future influences to avoid
5 Future influences to embrace

Example reading

1   2   3   4   5

1 I want to stop thinking about an ex who was dominant and controlling. I choose **the Emperor**.

2 Seven of Cups I'm kidding myself that maybe he/she will come back and everything will be different. What's stopping me is my overindulgence in my fantasies about how it all might have been different; the "if only" syndrome.

3 The Hanged Man I have to allow myself to feel the pain, grieve a little before I can move on, but also live for the moment and stop forcing myself to forget him/her, then it will just happen.

4 Four of Cups In the future I need to avoid feelings of apathy, emotional constipation, withholding affection from others because I can't trust anyone.

5 Five of Swords In the future I should put my needs first and look out for number one. Enjoy a few mind games with new people. Concentrate on what makes me feel good to be myself and consider that the end of this relationship was necessary for me to become myself.

Dumping doubts and fears

This spread is useful when you don't know what needs to be dumped, but you have a feeling that something isn't going right for you. It allows you to analyze yourself and see the best way to deal with current fears and doubts that are lurking in your psychological basement.

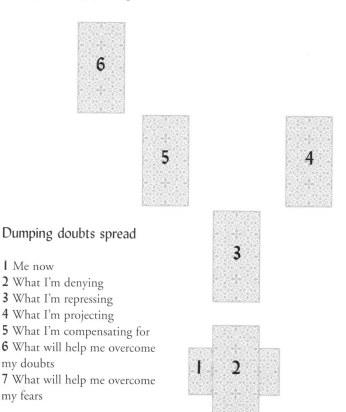

Dumping doubts spread

1 Me now
2 What I'm denying
3 What I'm repressing
4 What I'm projecting
5 What I'm compensating for
6 What will help me overcome my doubts
7 What will help me overcome my fears

Example reading

1 Ace of Cups I'm falling in love and it's scary.

2 Six of Wands Apparently this card suggests I don't feel good about myself, so how can anyone love me? That possibility just doesn't exist. What low self-esteem? Rubbish, I feel great. (In fact I'm in denial, I won't admit that actually I do have low self-esteem.)

3 Knight of Swords What I'm repressing is my desire to rush headlong into this relationship. I know I feel that way, but my inner judge says it's dangerous to leap in at the deep end, so I'll repress that desire.

4 The Emperor What I'm projecting right now is that I need to be in control. In fact, I'm convinced the person with whom I'm in love will probably try to control me if I get involved.

5 Three of Cups I'm compensating for my passionate feelings by playing it cool.

6 The Chariot What will help me overcome my self-doubt is to focus on what I want rather than what I fear.

7 Ace of Swords What will help me overcome those fears is to analyze the situation and see through my illusions. In fact, that's why I'm using this spread, so I can dump those doubts and fears and just enjoy being in love!

1   2   3   4   5   6   7

How do I find love?

Sometimes we are all alone and believe no one will ever love us. We surround ourselves with illusions about who we should be or how we should act so that we will be loved. In fact, we want to be anything other than ourselves. This spread allows you to explore what kind of love you need right now and how you will find it.

Find love spread

1 You now
2 The kind of love you need
3 What you must express
4 What you must give
5 What you must take
6 How you will find love

| 1 | 2 | 3 | 4 | 5 | 6 |

Example reading

1 Eight of Wands Everything is up in the air with you now, but you are desperate to be in a loving relationship.

2 King of Cups The kind of lover you need right now is a caring or emotionally healing person.

3 The Empress What you must express is your appreciation for beauty and nature. Unleash your innate sensuality.

4 Two of Pentacles What you must give is your fun-loving spirit.

5 Ten of Pentacles What you must take is the chance for long-term happiness.

6 The Hierophant You will find love through large groups of people, conventional belief systems, cultural events, further education.

Decision-maker

We all need to make decisions, but often put them off or vacillate between various solutions or choices. This spread opens your eyes to the various factors involved and points the way to the outcome of that decision. But it is up to you to make it.

Decision-maker spread

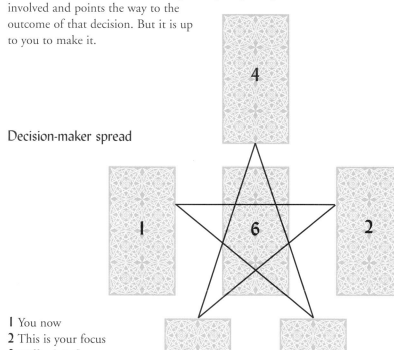

1 You now
2 This is your focus
3 Difficult influences
4 This makes sense
5 Unexpected insight
6 The outcome

| 1 | 2 | 3 | 4 | 5 | 6 |

Example reading

1 Ace of Wands You are fired up and eager to make a decision; you don't want to waste any time.

2 The High Priestess Focus on your intuition; it is probably on the mark right now.

3 Three of Pentacles Avoid involving other people in your decision making. Don't rely on teamwork.

4 Nine of Pentacles Self-reliance and sticking to your personal beliefs makes the most sense.

5 Page of Cups Unexpected insight will come from a younger friend, an attractive colleague, a gut reaction.

6 Strength The outcome will be that you have the inner strength to make a success of that decision.

Mystic seven

Based on the Celtic cross spread (see page 332), the Mystic Seven gives you insights into the past, present and future. It can be used for a straightforward analysis of what is going on in your life right now and the consequences of your intentions or actions.

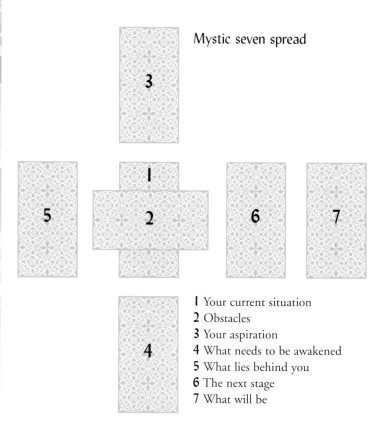

Mystic seven spread

1 Your current situation
2 Obstacles
3 Your aspiration
4 What needs to be awakened
5 What lies behind you
6 The next stage
7 What will be

| 1 | 2 | 3 | 4 | 5 | 6 | 7 |

Example reading

1 Five of Cups You are currently going through some kind of loss. This could be anything: money, a possession, work, an idea, a dream or a belief, a relationship. You have to deal with that loss, but something is obstructing you.

2 King of Swords The obstacle in your way is your own rigid values or a specific friend, partner or colleague/boss who has very high principles.

3 Page of Pentacles Your aspiration right now is for prosperity and practical results. You see yourself as worldly-wise.

4 Temperance What needs to be awakened is your ability to achieve equilibrium and harmony in all aspects of your life, not just material achievement.

5 Justice What lies behind you is that justice has been done.

6 Three of Cups The next stage is to branch out, to share your ideas, get together with new friends with whom you can form a bond or working unit.

7 The Fool The outcome is that you can set off on your own personal quest and be liberated from that sense of loss.

Divining myself

This is another solo spread to help you look within in order to get to know and understand yourself and your motivations.

Divining myself spread

1 I am this now
2 This is what bugs me
3 What I like about myself
4 What I don't like about myself
5 My talent
6 My temptation
7 My personal quest
8 My current guardian angel

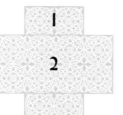

1 2 3 4

5 6 7 8

Example reading

1 The Magician Right now I'm taking action, I know what I'm doing and I'm good at it.

2 The Moon My fears and illusions bug me.

3 Two of Swords What I like about myself is my ability to keep cool when all around are in a flap. I'm self-contained.

4 Six of Cups What I don't like about myself is my sentimental side.

5 The Lovers My talent right now is having the conviction of my beliefs.

6 King of Wands My temptation is to show off.

7 Four of Swords My personal quest is to find some peace and be more laid-back about life.

8 Page of Swords My current guardian angel is truth, so I must face it.

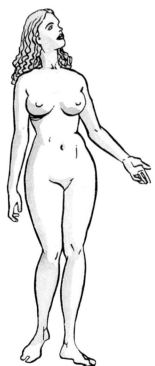

Aspirations and goals

Use this spread when you need motivation, self-belief and confidence to follow up your goals. You can also use it when you are not sure what direction to go in or if you are uncertain that the direction you have chosen is the right one.

Aspirations and goals spread

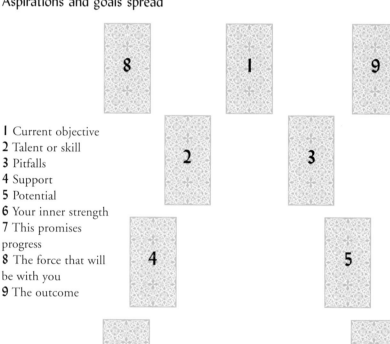

1 Current objective
2 Talent or skill
3 Pitfalls
4 Support
5 Potential
6 Your inner strength
7 This promises progress
8 The force that will be with you
9 The outcome

Example reading

1 Knight of Cups My current aspiration is to seduce someone.

2 Five of Wands My skill or talent is my sexy, provocative behavior.

3 The Tower The pitfall, however, is that it could all go terribly wrong if I'm too pushy.

4 Ace of Pentacles What will support me is being realistic about my limitations.

5 Six of Pentacles The potential is there to give and take a bit.

6 The Chariot My inner strength is my ability to let nothing distract me.

7 The High Priestess Being a little bit enigmatic will help.

8 Ten of Wands I must accept responsibility for my actions.

9 Queen of Cups The outcome looks to be emotional success and sexual happiness if I believe in myself.

Destiny spreads

How to use the destiny spreads

Most of these destiny spreads are based on traditional or more commonly used designs for divination. Use these spreads for looking in greater depth at issues and themes in the present, past and future.

By now you should know the best way to shuffle and how to chose random cards (go back to the "Getting started" chapter on pages 44–79 if you want to refresh your memory). Like all the other spreads in this book, lay the cards out in the order shown in the diagram, face down. Turn any reversed card into the upright position unless you want to use reversed cards (see pages 74–75).

Throughout the spreads there are example readings to give you guidance. Also remember that not all the spreads have "you now," "blockage" or "future

You hold your destiny in your hands.

outcome" positions which are referred to in the interpretations of each individual card. If you chose a layout that doesn't include these specific positions, interpret the card with its definitive meaning or develop the theme that surrounds the card to work it into the plot of the spread. Think how the lessons or knowledge revealed in these larger spreads can be applied to your current situation or your life journey.

You can use the traditional Celtic cross spread for any question or issue. This spread has become one of the most popular layouts among contemporary tarot readers.

The astrology-based spreads help you to project your ideas, needs and beliefs into the future, in order to see where to make changes or choices and adapt accordingly. We all want to "know" what the future holds because it makes us feel secure or that we are

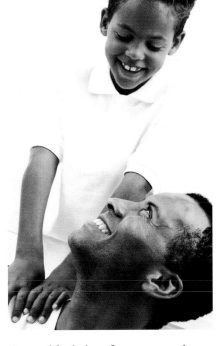

Create a lifestyle that reflects your true values.

in control of our lives. But this knowledge is, paradoxically, generated from your own inner desires and decisions. These spreads simply help to confirm exactly what is already inside you, what you want for your future, and to help you realize that destiny is your choice. As Carl Jung said, "a man's life is characteristic of himself."

Traditional Celtic cross

With this layout, ensure that you have an issue, theme or question that needs to be resolved, or use it to clarify where you are at any moment in time. Even if you only want some direction or objective perspective on your life journey, make sure you interpret each card in relation to your current situation.

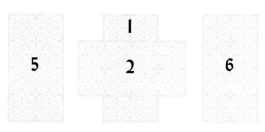

Celtic cross spread
1 You now/heart of the matter
2 Challenge/blockage
3 Conscious goal
4 Unknown influence
5 Past influence
6 Approaching influence
7 Inner resource or talent
8 How others see you
9 Hopes and/or fears
10 Outcome

| 1 | 2 | 3 | 4 | 5 | 6 | 7 |

Example reading

The issue: It feels as if things are going badly in my professional life. It seems as if no one is interested in my talents. What can I do?

| 8 | 9 | 10 |

1 Five of Pentacles I'm experiencing a sense of rejection and feeling insecure. I know there is something lacking in my life. I must accept it, but know it is probably only temporary.

2 Knight of Cups I am stopped from moving by having too many unrealistic or idealistic expectations.

3 The Empress My conscious goal is to be creative and to feel I'm being rewarded for my efforts.

4 The Chariot The positive unknown influence is my ability to keep working at it. I have the potential and talent.

5 Seven of Wands The past influence is that I remember how I defended my beliefs and ideas, and that this is imperative if I am to succeed.

6 Three of Pentacles The approaching influence is that I will soon be able to combine my talents with others.

7 Four of Swords My inner resource or talent is the ability to stand back from the situation and see it more objectively.

8 Five of Wands Others see me as competitive and rising to any challenge.

9 The Star I desperately hope to inspire others and want to feel wanted again.

10 Three of Cups With self-belief and realistic expectations, I'll soon be celebrating my success.

The zodiac

This spread, based on the 12 astrological signs and houses, gives you insight into all aspects of any current situation. Each position represents the qualities of the particular house and zodiac sign as you work round the horoscope. For example, the first card represents the first house of the zodiac, Aries; in other words, the way you view the world. The second house, Taurus, covers values, the third house, Gemini, communication and so on. For more information on the tarot and the zodiac, see pages 356–363.

The zodiac spread

1 My window on the world (1st house, Aries)
2 What I value most right now (2nd house, Taurus)
3 What I need to communicate (3rd house, Gemini)
4 My sense of belonging (4th house, Cancer)
5 How I can feel special (5th house, Leo)
6 Where I can be of service (6th house, Virgo)
7 What makes me feel complete (7th house, Libra)
8 My sexual needs (8th house, Scorpio)
9 What gives my life meaning (9th house, Sagittarius)
10 How I appear to the world (10th house, Capricorn)
11 My current ideals (11th house, Aquarius)
12 My secret (12th house, Pisces)

Example reading

1 Queen of Wands I see the world through a cheerful eye. I'm optimistic and loaded with enthusiasm for everything new.

2 The Hierophant I value education and knowledge more than anything else.

3 The Devil I need to talk about money and power.

4 Six of Pentacles I get a sense of belonging with those who are generous.

5 Eight of Wands How can I feel special? Engage in meaningful conversations, put my plans into action.

6 The Hermit I can be of service by helping others.

7 Two of Cups A close bond with someone makes me feel complete.

8 Nine of Cups My sexual needs are sensually indulgent right now.

9 Queen of Swords I can find a meaning in life through understanding human nature.

10 Ace of Cups I appear to the world as if I'm emotionally secure.

11 The Sun My current ideals are for personal success and greater insight.

12 Ten of Wands My current secret is that I feel tied down by responsibilities and would love to lighten my load.

Astrology see-saw

For this spread the cards are read in pairs to allow you to see both sides of the issues that affect us all. How do you balance your personal inner world with the apparent outer one? Are your individual values in accord with any joint financial issues? Are your emotional needs being met by your work or career in the big wide world? Are your individual goals being distorted by collective expectations? How do you balance the routines and rituals of ordinary life with your spiritual hopes, dreams and secret desires?

Astrology see-saw spread
1 and 2 Who you are, what you project on others
3 and 4 Personal value, joint resources
5 and 6 Current focus, meaning in life
7 and 8 Emotional need, outer image/success
9 and 10 Individual goal, collective expectation
11 and 12 Day-to-day reality, your secret world

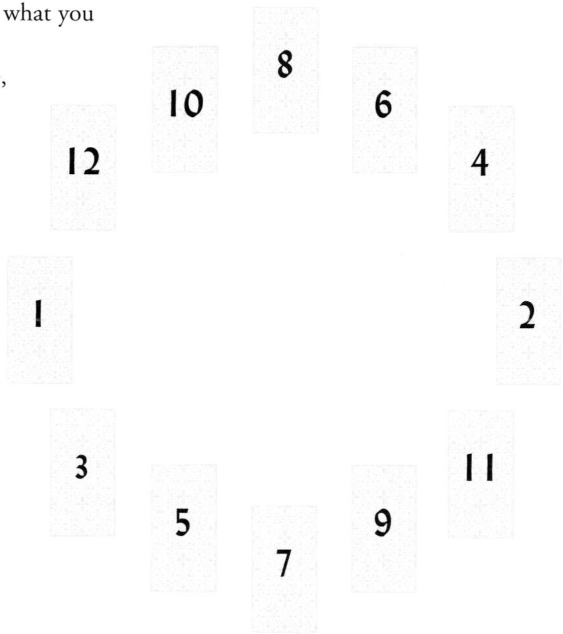

8

10   6

12   4

1   2

3   11

5   9

7

1   2   3   4   5   6   7

8   9   10   11   12

Example reading

1 and 2 Six of Swords, Knight of Wands

Currently I'm moving out of a rut, I'm leaving behind some bad times and feel more positive about where I'm going, but it's hard work. Everyone seems to be hot-tempered, brash and rash and more interested in themselves than in me. What am I projecting? My own desire for a passionate lifestyle. Better "own" that projection and get on with it!

3 and 4 The Hierophant, the Queen of Wands My personal values are very conventional; right now I conform to the rulebook where money is concerned. This is harmonious with joint resources. My partner/business colleague and I are wholeheartedly enthusiastic about being creative with our finances.

5 and 6 Seven of Swords, the World At the moment I'm a bit of an intellectual lone wolf and keep things to myself. The World suggests that I need to expand my horizons rather than be narrow-minded.

7 and 8 The Moon, Two of Wands Emotionally I'm a little lost, a bit scared deep down inside; I present a bold, commanding outer image to disguise my vulnerability. I must not neglect my needs for the sake of personal power-tripping.

9 and 10 Ace of Cups, the Lovers I would love to be more self-sufficient but everyone sees me as part of a couple.

11 and 12 Ten of Cups, Four of Pentacles On the surface I lead a conventional life, but in my heart I wish I was free from material gain.

The gypsy

This spread provides a colorful palette from which to thread together your past, present and future. Often used by gypsy fortune-tellers in the past, this is one of the most detailed layouts and covers all aspects of your life.

Note: You can either read this layout one line of cards at a time to cover the past, present or future from left to right, or read them in columns as themes: work—past, present and future; home—past, present, future; and so on as outlined here.

	I	II	III	IV	V	VI	VII
C	15	16	17	18	19	20	21
B	8	9	10	11	12	13	14
A	1	2	3	4	5	6	7

The gypsy spread

A The past
B The present
C The future

I Work/prospects
II Home/needs
III Luck/desires
IV Friends/support
V Love/sex
VI Plans/goals
VII Personal quest

Example readings

Work (I)

1 The Fool In the past I took a chance to get where I am now.

8 Seven of Pentacles In the present I must find time to take stock and reevaluate where I'm going.

15 Six of Cups In the future a creative

1 **8** **15**

period is coming up and I'll really be able to enjoy the fruits of my labor.

Home/needs (II)

2 Knight of Swords In the past, I've been very insensitive to someone else's needs, only thinking of myself.

9 Four of Pentacles Right now I'm clinging to the known, because it feels safer/I don't want to move home.

2 **9** **16**

16 Ten of Swords Soon I'll realize how over the top I'm being about it all. Things are beginning to look up.

Luck/desires (III)

3 Ten of Cups In the past I was really happy, had a good family life and got what I wanted.

10 Five of Wands Right now it seems as if everything is a hassle; there is always opposition to my desires.

3 **10** **17**

17 The Tower Soon, I'm going to see the truth, realize that it's time to wake up and get out of a rut.

The year ahead

This spread is based on the astrological year rather than
the calendar year. The astrological year begins at
0 degrees Aries, and as Aries corresponds to most of April,
your first card represents April, the second May and so on.

Lay the cards out in this way, but start reading from the card
that represents the month you are actually in at the moment. For
example, if it is early June when you do the spread, you would start reading
from the third card and so on.

The year ahead spread

Opportunities and/or
mission for each month

1 April
2 May
3 June
4 July
5 August
6 September
7 October
8 November
9 December
10 January
11 February
12 March

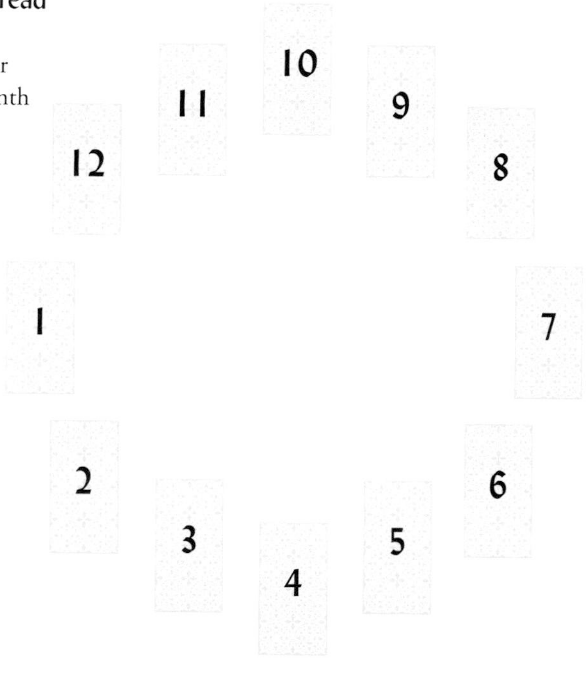

| 3 | 4 | 5 | 6 | 7 | 8 | 9 |

Example reading

3 June **The Empress** Maternal issues—pregnancy, creativity, feeling connected to nature. Mission is to give birth to something!

4 July **Six of Wands** Opportunity to achieve some kind of success. Don't get on your high horse, though.

5 August **The Lovers** Relationships will be important. You will be on a crusade for passion.

6 September **Judgement** You have the chance to start afresh or recognize your true vocation.

7 October **Four of Pentacles** Financial opportunities. Take care that you are not controlling or possessive.

8 November **King of Swords** Get to know someone with high standards, or a good communicator. They could be useful to you.

9 December **Ten of Pentacles** Your plans for the future start to take off. You are having a run of good fortune; don't give up on your plans.

The chakras

Eastern spiritual traditions maintain that a system of energy flows through the body linked by seven main energy centres known as chakras. Sometimes we intuitively know that this energy flow isn't in balance, that something is wrong; we can't progress with our career or never seem to find the perfect partner. By using the tarot you can determine which chakra might be blocked and what might be the underlying cause for your imbalance.

This spread is also great for discovering where any unknown psychological blockage is and what therefore needs to be expressed or worked through.

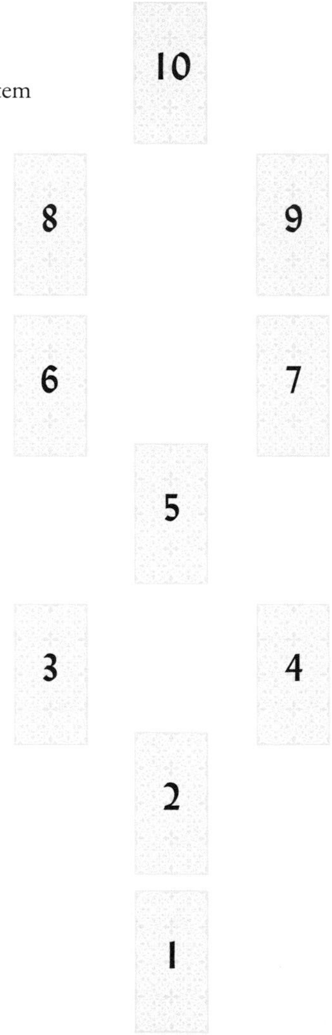

10

8   9

6   7

5

The chakra spread

3   4

1 Base or Root Chakra
2 Sacral Chakra
3 and 4 Solar Plexus Chakra
5 Heart Chakra
6 and 7 Throat Chakra
8 and 9 Third Eye Chakra
10 Crown Chakra

2

1

| 1 | 2 | 3 | 4 | 5 | 6 | 7 |

Example reading

The sample reading below gives cards and interpretations for only the first four chakras, but defines the area of concern for all seven.

| 8 | 9 | 10 |

I am feeling very negative about everything right now.

1 The Root Chakra is concerned with your sense of groundedness and basic survival instinct. **Queen of Swords** Currently I'm alert and well grounded mentally, so what is the problem?

2 The Sacral Chakra is concerned with sexuality and feelings. **The Devil** I'm chained to my illusions. Does this chakra need to be cleansed? Perhaps I'm not expressing my sexual or emotional needs to someone.

3 and 4 The Solar Plexus Chakra is concerned with the state of your ego. **Ten of Cups, Nine of Pentacles** My outer ego is fairly strong but I must make a commitment to sort out my inner world.

5 The Heart Chakra is concerned with compassion and self-nurture. **Nine of Cups** I'm fairly self-reliant, but I'm not really concerned about other people's feelings; maybe I should be more loving and that will help to heal my own negativity. This is the real source of my problem.

6 and 7 The Throat Chakra is concerned with how you communicate.

8 and 9 The Third Eye Chakra is concerned with insights and intellectual processes.

10 The Crown Chakra is where you connect to the divine; it is concerned with your high spiritual self.

Projection

The qualities or issues you unconsciously or consciously project onto the world around you are revealed in this spread. An example of projection is when you don't realize that you have the talent to sing, so you fall in love with a rock star who acts out your own singing talent for you. It works in a negative, shadowy way too; for example, you may hate people who make jokes all the time. Recognize that perhaps it is the joker in you that needs to be expressed. **Note:** You should use only the Major Arcana and the court cards with this spread for a deeper interpretation.

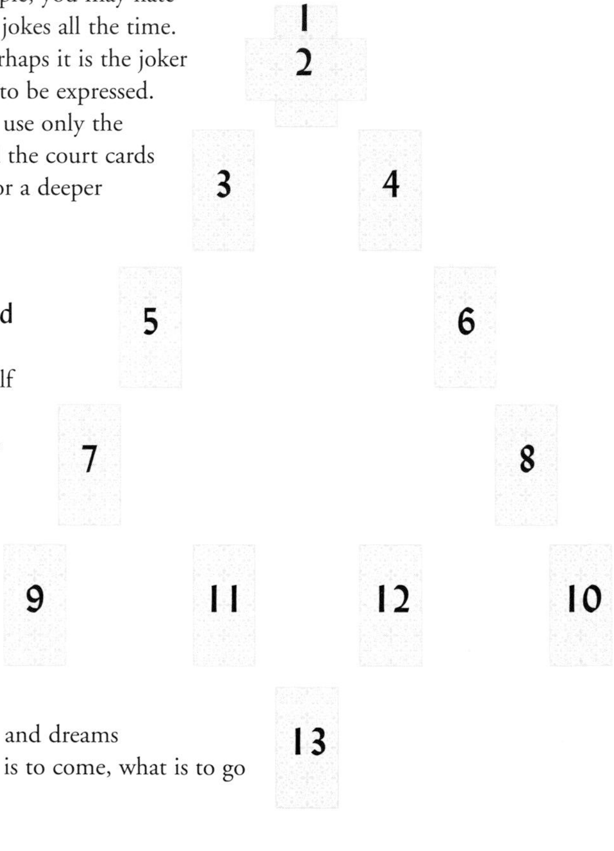

1

2

3

4

Projection spread

5

6

1 How I see myself right now

2 What I can't see about myself

3 and 4 Tests and boundaries

5 and 6 People and relationships

7 and 8 Goals and ideals

9 and 10 Desires and dreams

11 and 12 What is to come, what is to go

13 Outcome

7

8

9

11

12

10

13

1   2   3   4   5   6   7

8   9   10   11   12   13

Example reading

1 Page of Wands I see myself as a free spirit, enthusiastic and able to do almost anything.

2 Queen of Pentacles What I don't see is that I'm always trying to make everyone else happy and not myself.

3 and 4 Wheel of Fortune, the Hermit I need to take a risk, make choices and move on.

5 and 6 Emperor, Knight of Cups I attract powerful people into my life right now. Am I expressing my own power? Do I believe in the perfect partner? What does that tell me about my own sense of perfection or inadequacy?

7 and 8 The Chariot, Queen of Wands To achieve my goals I'll have to express this independent spirit, rather than let others act it out for me.

9 and 10 The Tower, Page of Swords I must do something positive rather than projecting my desire for change onto others.

11 and 12 The Lovers, Hanged Man What is to come—taking responsibility for my choices; what is to go—being dependent on others for my happiness.

13 Strength I will have the strength and courage to make the changes necessary to achieve my goals.

The wish-list

With this spread you will discover how to make your
dream future come true. Different from most of the
other spreads, in this instance you choose the first seven
cards yourself. Look through the pack and decide which one
you feel is relevant to each of your future dreams or
wishes. How do you see yourself in a year's time?

Do think about these ideas clearly before you
start choosing cards. It doesn't matter which
cards you choose as long as you "feel" they
represent or indicate that particular desire or
wish. Everything is possible and you can make
dreams real if you truly believe in yourself. So what is
the ideal you—single but surrounded by a host of friends, or married and
starting a family? In a high-powered profession or an alternative lifestyle?

Choose the last seven cards at random after shuffling the deck and holding
it face down. As you place the randomly selected cards next to your chosen
cards they will give you the insight or direction needed to make those
dreams come true.

Wish-list spread

1 My ideal future is . . .
2 Where I want to be this time next year
3 Who I want to be with this time next year
4 Family or independence?
5 What I want to achieve
6 What I want to learn
7 What I want to leave behind
8, 9, 10, 11, 12, 13, 14 Insights into making these wishes come true

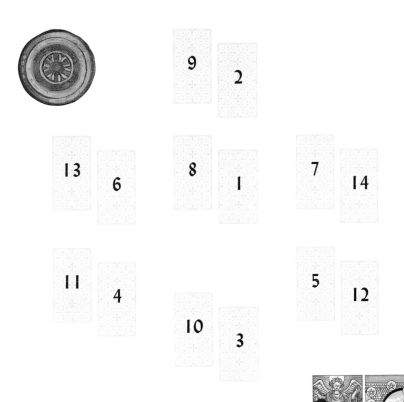

9
2
13
6
8
1
7
14
11
4
10
3
5
12

Example reading

1 Say you chose **the Lovers** for "your ideal future." You want the perfect relationship and to be in love. How to make it real? Well, the card you randomly choose for position eight will give you an insight into how to make this real; say you randomly choose **Ten of Pentacles**.

1   8

This means that you will realize your ideal future through conventional associations, material and financial institutions, organizations or business associations where you'll find yourself in the perfect relationship.

Developing skills
and knowledge

Going deeper

Once you are a little more familiar with the tarot cards, you can start to widen your knowledge by combining other divination techniques to add extra elements to your readings. The tarot has close associations with astrology, the Kabbalah and numerology. These ancient arts are all part of the same tapestry threaded with the rich symbols and archetypal energies which permeate life.

You can introduce any of these extra skills to your readings at any time. You might find that some are not suited to your personal work, and others are simply a nuisance, getting in the way of the clarity that is the tarot. But it is very useful to see how these correspondences work. Meditation is also a great

way to learn about the tarot from a different perspective and it allows you to enter the world of tarot rather than feel that you are a watcher standing outside it, observing a life that is not your own.

Creating your own spreads is also very important in developing your skills as a reader. This enables you to play with numbers and geometry, the vital keys to symbol interpretation. You increase your skills and set questions and statements that come from the heart, rather than merely out of a textbook.

Finally, the short section on working with others helps you learn how to share your ideas, and to understand how you operate in a small group, the archetypal realm of the tarot working through the collective rather than just the individual.

Tarot magic

Choose the card that most closely corresponds with the spell you want to perform. Light a candle and place it next to the card face up. Concentrate on the card for a few minutes, repeat its name three times and the spell is then cast.

Cards and candles for spells

CARD	CANDLE	SPELLS
The Fool	White	For new beginnings, children, creativity
The Magician	Yellow	For communication, protection against deception
The High Priestess	Lavender	For secrets, women, spirituality
The Empress	Pink	For marriage, fertility, loyalty, trust
The Emperor	Dark blue	For success, empowerment, career issues
The Hierophant	Purple	For wisdom, finding lost objects
The Lovers	Green	For love spells, sex, romance
The Chariot	Bright red	For travel, moving home, self-confidence
Strength	Dark red	For patience, overcoming limitations
The Hermit	Silver	For personal integrity
The Wheel of Fortune	Orange	For money matters, good fortune
Justice	Gray	For decision-making, negotiations
The Hanged Man	Dark green	For self-acceptance, giving up addictions
Death	Dark brown	For dumping emotional baggage, fresh starts
Temperance	Lilac	For calm feelings, new perspective, cooling ardor
The Devil	Ochre	For overcoming fear and self-doubt
The Tower	Vanilla	For property, sexuality, protection
The Star	Pale yellow	For fame, recognition
The Moon	Jasmine	For beauty, peace, attraction
The Sun	Gold	For happiness, energy, creativity
Judgement	Indigo	For forgiveness, breaking free
The World	Multicolored	For self-confidence, new ideas, travel

Numerology

Many ancient cultures believed in the significance and power of numbers, particularly the Greeks and Hebrews, who developed the systems used in modern-day numerology.

The Greek mathematician and philosopher Pythagorus wrote in the 6th century B.C.E. that "numbers are the first things of all of nature." His theory was that everything was symbolized or brought back down to a single digit number. Numbers weren't just of mathematical significance, but were central to everything that went on in the universe. They were the key to all wisdom. The primary numbers one to nine each vibrate to a different frequency, and these vibrations echo throughout the universe. This "music of the spheres" was an expression of the heavenly bodies, which had their own numerical value and harmonic vibration. Various symbols are used by different cultures to symbolize the numbers, but the Pythagorean system, based on the nine primary numbers, is the most common.

Numerology and the tarot

The tarot is rich with numerical significance and value. The Major Arcana consists of a strange number of cards to have—why 22 cards? The number 22 is said to be the most perfectly balanced number. It is said to embody spiritual evolution, worldly success, the coming together of reason, intellect, vision, feeling and skill. It combines all of these elements in its balance.

Note that the court cards of each suit are usually given values as follows: Page = 4, Knight = 3, Queen = 2, King = 1.

Page **(four)**   *Knight* **(three)**   *Queen* **(two)**   *King* **(one)**

Using numbers for tarot readings

Because each tarot card has its own number, you can use these in two different ways to create another dimension to your reading. By adding together all the numbers of the chosen cards in a spread and reducing them down to a single digit, you can obtain information about the overall *long-term* direction of a reading. This *Quintessential Number* is the overall guide and purpose of the reading in question.

Say you choose the Six of Wands, the King of Swords, the Magician and the Empress in a spread. Their values are:

$6 + 1 + 1 + 3 = 11$
$1 + 1 = 2$

The Quintessential Number is 2

Specific dates

You can also combine the tarot and numerology for checking out special dates, to find out which of several days is the most auspicious for organizing an event, meeting up with a new admirer or simply a good day to send out that resumé.

If you have an important day you want to check out, write down the numbers and add them up. Jane wanted her wedding on July 17, 2007. Her mother suggested July 3 and her her mother-in-law suggested August 9. She wrote down the three numbers in numerical format:

$1 + 7 + 7 + 2 + 7 = 24$
$2 + 4 = 6$

$3 + 7 + 2 + 7 = 19$
$1 + 9 = 10 = 1$

$9 + 8 + 2 + 7 = 26$
$2 + 6 = 8$

In order to find out the best day, Jane shuffled the pack and then drew the sixth card that was face down from the top of the pile, followed by the first card (obviously the next one) from the top, followed by the 8th card from the top. She then read the interpretations for each card to determine which date was the best for her wedding. You can do the same for any dates that you have.

What will happen on this day?

If you ask questions surrounding a specific date, for example, "I'm going to start my new job on February 23, 2007, what can I expect on that day? What is the long-term direction of this?", you can use the tarot card you picked randomly as an answer for the first question and then the Quintessential Number as the answer for the second question. The date in question is February 23, 2007:

2 + 3 + 2 + 7 = 14 = 5

Add this number to your date of birth, for example, March 9, 1970:

9 + 3 + 1 + 9 + 7 = 29 = 11 = 2
5 + 2 = 7

Draw the seventh card from the top of the pack after shuffling the deck to discover what you can expect on that day. Next, look up the number seven in the numerological interpretations above to discover what the long-term outlook is.

What each Quintessential Number means

NUMBER	MEANING
One	The number of action. Single-minded, independent, the number one informs you that you must be innovative and motivated to succeed in your plans.
Two	The number of negotiation. Cooperative and laid-back, this number is telling you to adapt to circumstances to fulfill your dream.
Three	The number of communication. Express yourself through a creative outlet and your life journey will benefit from fun-loving relationships.
Four	The number of realistic thinking. If you are practical and self-reliant, you will have the motivation to achieve whatever you set out to do, and can turn any situation to your advantage.
Five	The number of creative adventure. It is time to be more outgoing, exploring, and questioning of others' motives. The expressive side of your nature will enable you to make changes to suit you.
Six	The number of the protector. It is time be of service in some way to bring out your nurturing side. However, six also reminds you not to let others decide your future for you.
Seven	The number of mysticism. On your life journey you will encounter many people involved in healing. You have an extraordinary talent for understanding the world. Listen to your intuition for the answer to a current dilemma.
Eight	The number of ambition. Right now you have a secret inner drive for success and power. And you'll feel cheated if you don't achieve material results. Plan ahead, sort out finances and the results will be equal to your goal.
Nine	The number of vision. You have extraordinary vision for the future, but following things through will be hard. You must try to avoid making promises you can't fulfill, then you will gain the top prize.

Astrology and the tarot

The tarot embodies a rich source of astrological correspondences, and when combined they provide a deeper understanding of yourself and the reading in question.

Each card in the Major Arcana corresponds to a specific sun-sign or planet of the zodiac system. Knowledge of these correspondences may give added emphasis and information to any reading. For example, if your "you now" card is the World, you can see this corresponds to Capricorn. The additional interpretation for Capricorn can give you added insights into the meaning of the card. Whether you are born a Capricorn or not, this card is also asking "what qualities of Capricorn are lacking or overemphasized in your life right now?"

By reading these sun-sign and planet correspondences you can gain further insight into your current issue. Develop these ideas further by looking at more detailed information about the qualities of the planets and sun-signs in astrological literature.

Sun-signs and their associated Major Arcana cards

	SIGN	CARD
♈	Aries	The Emperor
♉	Taurus	The Hierophant
♊	Gemini	The Lovers
♋	Cancer	The Chariot
♌	Leo	Strength
♍	Virgo	The Hermit
♎	Libra	Justice
♏	Scorpio	Death
♐	Sagittarius	Temperance
♑	Capricorn	The Devil
♒	Aquarius	The Star
♓	Pisces	The Moon

Planets and their associated Major Arcana cards

	PLANET	CARD
☉	Sun	The Sun
☽	Moon	The High Priestess
☿	Mercury	The Magician
♀	Venus	The Empress
♂	Mars	The Tower
♃	Jupiter	Wheel of Fortune
♄	Saturn	The World
♅	Uranus	The Fool
♆	Neptune	The Hanged Man
♇	Pluto	Judgement

Sun-sign card interpretations

Use the following interpretations to add a further dimension to your tarot readings.

Aries and the Emperor

Aries is about asserting yourself, taking control of your life, showing who is the boss. Being single-minded will get you ahead now, but, if you identify or associate already with this energy or know you are expressing it, then take care that you don't push others too far.

Taurus and the Hierophant

Taurus needs to feel secure. When you draw this card, think about whether you are needy, possessive or materialistically driven to succeed. If you are already expressing this energy, then avoid becoming too fanatical about your goal. If you feel this energy is lacking, you need to rely more on the facts and develop an inner sense of security.

Gemini and the Lovers

Gemini relies on wits and brains. So are you using your head to make a decision, or relying on your heart? If you aren't expressing this energy then it is time to utilize your logic. If your mind is working overtime, then perhaps you need to get in touch with your heart.

Cancer and the Chariot

Cancer wants to belong. When you draw the Chariot do you feel you belong to anything or anyone—a tribe, a clan, family, lover, circle of friends or institution? Do you cling desperately to anyone or anything for fear of being alone? Don't hide your true feelings. If this energy is lacking, then it is time to embrace someone and feel you belong in the big wide world. If you want to break free, do so.

Leo and Strength

Leo wants to be special. When you draw Strength, are you under the spotlight, do you like being the center of attention? Or do you feel left out in the cold or immune to praise? If this quality is lacking in your life, your own talents and gifts will now bring you the attention you deserve. If this quality is overflowing, then take care that you don't assume the spotlight is only on you.

Virgo and the Hermit

Virgo is discriminating but critical. When you draw the Hermit ask yourself if you are being too self-critical, or are you making too many demands on yourself and others? If you feel this energy is lacking, you may need to allow yourself more time to put your life into perspective.

Libra and Justice

Libra seeks balance and diplomacy. If this energy is strong for you now, too much compromise means that you are giving up on your own beliefs or opinions just to make others happy. If you believe it is lacking, learn diplomacy to resolve a dilemma and be more civilized about life.

Scorpio and Death

Scorpio is about passion and power. When you draw Death, the astrological aspect of this card is the power to transform your life—to end one cycle that is not working for you and begin again. But if you identify too easily with this card, check that you are not wielding power for the sake of it.

Sagittarius and Temperance

Sagittarius is optimistic and explorative. When you draw Temperance, you have the chance to work on your desires and take the road toward achieving your goals. If you identify too easily with this energy, then moderate your plans, rethink and reformulate before rushing headlong into something new.

Capricorn and the Devil

Capricorn is self-reliant and conventional. Are you currently following traditional rules about how to act, behave or love to such a rigid degree that you are denying your true feelings? Don't let dark thoughts get to you; it is time to stand up for individual rights, too.

Aquarius and the Star

Aquarius is idealistic and independent. When you draw the Star and you feel this energy is lacking in your life, it is time to believe in yourself and trust in doing things your way. If you identify too readily with this independent energy, then take care that you are not trying to influence others without a thought for their personal needs.

Pisces and the Moon

Pisces is impressionable. If you identify with this energy, are you currently being misled by what others say, do, or believe, or can you see beyond the empty promises? Are you trying too hard to make someone happy? If you believe this quality is lacking in your life, it's time to be more in touch with your intuition and your feelings.

The planets

The Sun (rules Leo)

Tarot card: the Sun

The astrological Sun card tells you to act positively and with complete confidence in your abilities. But take care that you are not being arrogant or selfish.

The Moon (rules Cancer)

Tarot card: the High Priestess

The astrological High Priestess tells you to listen to your intuition, to wait for the right moment to act and not to be swayed by others' opinions.

Mercury (rules Gemini and Virgo)
Tarot card: the Magician

The astrological Magician tells you to watch out for dishonesty or trickery from others. Be wise enough to see ahead and make plans accordingly.

Venus (rules Taurus and Libra)
Tarot card: the Empress

The astrological Empress tells you to think about your true values. Are you living a lie, or is it doing things and being with people that make you happy?

Mars (rules Aries)
Tarot card: the Tower

The astrological Tower tells you it's time to shake up the status quo. Get out and do your own thing, and throw aside any limitations imposed on you by others.

Jupiter (rules Sagittarius)
Tarot card: the Wheel of Fortune

The astrological Wheel of Fortune tells you to take advantage of any new or unexpected opportunities. Widen your perspective and move on while you can.

Saturn (rules Capricorn)
Tarot card: the World

The astrological World tells you to face reality, to put your feet on the ground and accept what is possible and what is not. You can achieve much, but you have to work hard at it. You can't have your cake and eat it.

Uranus (rules Aquarius)
Tarot card: the Fool

The astrological Fool tells you to move forward and try a new direction, even if it seems a little risky. This is your chance to do your own thing and leap ahead.

Neptune (rules Pisces)
Tarot card: the Hanged Man

The astrological Hanged Man tells you it is time to relinquish your attachment to things or people which serve no purpose to you. You have a life, so live it.

Pluto (rules Scorpio)
Tarot card: Judgment

The astrological Judgment card says it is time to let go of the past, to forget your petty resentments and embrace the future. Make the change now while you can and feel liberated.

Developing skills and knowledge

Kaballah

The Kabbalah is an ancient esoteric and magical pathway from the Hebrew tradition that offers profound wisdom and spiritual insight. The word *kabbalah* is derived from a Hebrew word meaning "to receive." The core element of the Kabbalah is the Tree of Life, a blueprint for the universe which attempts to reveal the interconnected aspects of all life.

In the mid-nineteenth century, Eliphas Levi (born Alphonse Louis Constant), an ex-Catholic priest turned teacher and writer, made the first connections between the Kabbalah and the tarot. He noticed that the 22 Major Arcana cards seemed to correspond to the 22 letters of the Hebrew alphabet which were part of the pathways of the Tree of Life. These letters and pathways subsequently connected each card with specific ways to enlightenment. Levi also linked the rest of the tarot pack to other aspects of the Tree of Life.

Even in its simplest form, the Tree of Life can form a powerful blueprint for a personal divination system when used with the tarot. There is not enough room in this book to go into the more profound elements of using the Kabbalah. But the following correspondences and Tree of Life layout using the tarot will deepen your knowledge.

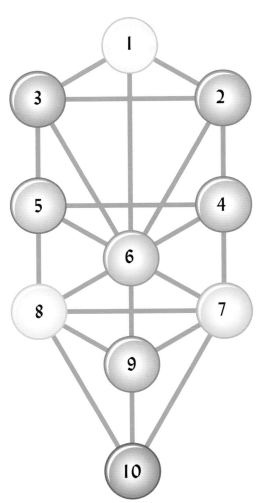

The Tree of Life

1 Kether (Unity)
2 Chokmah (Wisdom)
3 Binah (Understanding)
4 Chesed (Gifts)
5 Geburah (Challenges)
6 Tiphareth (The heart of the problem)
7 Netzach (Desires/feelings)
8 Hod (Intellect)
9 Yesod (The unconscious)
10 Malkuth (Environment/outcome)

The Minor Arcana

The ten circular "spheres" numbered one through ten on the Tree of Life are related to the numbered pip cards. In other words, Sphere One relates to the Aces, Sphere Two to the twos, Sphere Three to the Threes and so on. The court cards are represented at each level, so the Kings and Queens are at Spheres Two and Three, Knights at Sphere Six, and Pages or Princesses at Sphere Ten.

The Major Arcana

The Spheres are connected by 22 lines or pathways. These pathways each have one letter of the Hebrew alphabet assigned to them and each path has an association with one of the Major Arcana cards. If you would like further information on using the pathways, there are many specialized books on the tarot and Kaballah available.

Daath

There is also an invisible sphere midway between Kether and Tiphareth, called Daath. You can also use this as a placement in readings, but take care because it represents Hidden Knowledge or the Abyss, which separates the finite from the infinite and the Divine from the human.

If you use this placement in your layout, it reveals your deeper motives, what is going on in your unconscious, the realm between reality and illusion. This knowledge cannot be used for material or personal gain, but only for greater self-awareness.

Tree of Life reading

Use this spread when you are in need of life direction or personal development. Read the spread from bottom to top; just go with the flow of the layout and focus on the strengths and weaknesses of each card in its relevant position.

Now read the spread from top to bottom, in what is referred to as a "Lightning Flash" reading. Without analyzing or trying to interpret each card, just look at them in relation to one another; see them as interconnected to each other, and you should suddenly have a "flash of insight" into the real meaning of this spread for you. This may not happen the first time you do it, so don't push yourself. It is the power of the Tree of Life's secret that will enable you to see through the illusions of your current problem to the real truth of the matter.

Tree of Life spread

1 Kether (Unity)
2 Chokmah (Wisdom)
3 Binah (Understanding)
4 Chesed (Gifts)
5 Geburah (Challenges)
6 Tiphareth (The heart of the problem)
7 Netzach (Desires/feelings)
8 Hod (Intellect)
9 Yesod (The unconscious)
10 Malkuth (Environment/outcome)

 10

 8   9

 6   7

 5

 4   3

2

 1

Crystals

As long ago as 4000 B.C.E., the Chaldean people of Mesopotamia believed that crystals found in the earth were linked to the planets, and in turn reflected the vibrations of the cosmos. From earliest times crystals have been thought to have divinatory powers.

By correspondence, each crystal aligns to one of the energies associated to each tarot card, specifically the Major Arcana. Throughout history crystals have been used in fortune-telling for their subtle vibrational nature, thought to be linked to the vibrational powers of the cosmos. As a divinatory tool, they can be laid out in simple spreads of one, two or three crystals, similar to any of the tarot card layouts.

The crystals that correspond to each of the 22 Major Arcana are outlined in the chart on the opposite page. You don't have to use these specific crystals, though; feel free to create your own tarot crystal set in the following way.

Take 22 crystals of varying kinds that you truly like and place them in your crystal bag and shake gently. Next, take the 22 Major Arcana cards from the pack, shuffle them and pick one at random, then place it face down on the table. Randomly pick a crystal from the bag and place it on top of the face-down card. Do this until you have one crystal on top of each card.

Turn over the cards one by one and place each crystal above the card. Make a note of each crystal that corresponds to each Major Arcana card. Write them down because it's easy to forget to begin with. Spend time every day getting to know the meaning behind your crystals when merged with that of the tarot card it represents.

Crystals and the Major Arcana

CARD	CRYSTAL	KEY WORD
The Fool	Orange Carnelian	Rebellion
The Magician	Topaz	Understanding
The High Priestess	Opal	Sensitivity
The Empress	Tourmaline	Compassion
The Emperor	Red Carnelian	Action
The Hierophant	Rose Quartz	Value
The Lovers	Citrine	Communication
The Chariot	Moonstone	Control
Strength	Tiger's Eye	Inspiration
The Hermit	Peridot	Discrimination
The Wheel of Fortune	Lapis Lazuli	Wisdom
Justice	Jade	Harmony
The Hanged Man	Blue Lace Agate	Sacrifice
Death	Malachite	Transformation
Temperance	Turquoise	Going with the flow
The Devil	Obsidian	Breaking free
The Tower	Red Agate	Progression
The Star	Amber	Rationalization
The Moon	Aquamarine	Fantasy
The Sun	Clear Quartz	Optimism
Judgement	Amethyst	Awakening
The World	Onyx	Structure

Crystal empowerment

You can empower any crystal with the essence of a particular tarot archetype. This energizes the crystal with specific powers for a short-term or permanent effect. As when you hold a crystal in your hand to draw in its energy or to give your own out, the tarot archetype is infused into the crystal so that, when you carry it or wear it, you are carrying the card's psychic energy.

Step-by-step guide

1 Decide which card is the most appropriate for your purpose, and acknowledge that this purpose is for the benefit of all. Maybe you are seeking new romance, so you might use the Lovers.

2 Place the crystal of your choice on the card, and repeat the card's name three times (the Lovers, the Lovers, the Lovers), and ask for the card's essence to enter the crystal for your specific purpose.

3 For a more long-term infusion —say you wanted to find a spiritual pathway that worked for you and wanted affirmation of that in the future—leave the card and the crystal overnight on your window ledge on the night of a full moon. It doesn't matter if the sky is cloudy.

Tarot essences for crystal empowerment

Here is a brief guide to the tarot archetypes. However, read the interpretations of each card as well to give you extra insight into the energy you want to reinforce in your life.

CARD	INTERPRETATION
The Fool	New journey, exploration, free spirit, trusting the universe
The Magician	Focus, magic, communication, intellect
The High Priestess	Clairvoyance, inner guidance, psychic energy, deeper wisdom
The Empress	Nurturing, grounding, creativity, new life
The Emperor	Authority, asserting yourself, new projects
The Hierophant	Centering, teaching, transmitting ideas
The Lovers	Love relationships, making choices, balancing energy
The Chariot	Domestic happiness, knowing where you are going
Strength	Courage, self-confidence, making a dream come true
The Hermit	Spiritual enlightenment or direction, inner peace, patience
Wheel of Fortune	Taking chances, being inspired, luck, change
Justice	Clarity, legal or financial affairs, agreements, making compromises
The Hanged Man	Mystical empowerment, seeing the truth, giving up bad habits
Death	New beginnings, transformation, dumping emotional baggage
Temperance	Balanced relationships, freedom yet commitment, self-belief
The Devil	Sexual vitality, sexual attraction
The Tower	Breaking down bad habits, purging your feelings, emotional breakthrough
The Star	Meditation, spiritual guidance, freedom, intellectual wisdom
The Moon	Relationship magic, dream work, for deeper understanding, to keep a secret
The Sun	For discovering the truth, creativity, success, childbirth
Judgement	Transitions, new perception, transformation
The World	Journeys, integration, completion, fulfillment

Psychology and archetypes

Archetypes are at the core of all symbolic divination systems, and are particularly important in the tarot. The great early twentieth-century psychologist Carl Jung coined the word "archetype" which is defined as those instinctual forces or patterns of behavior that operate in the depths of the human psyche and are universal.

These archetypes work within our psyche rather like our bodily instincts work in the physical body. When we feel physically or emotionally threatened, our adrenaline levels shoot up, the "fight or flight" response mechanism kicks into life, and we respond. This isn't something we have consciously decided. We cannot see these instincts nor can we see archetypes. And we won't have much control over the more shadowy patterns that keep repeating themselves in our lives unless we become more aware of these forces that erupt from our psychological basement.

These archetypes do change in description depending on the culture or social climate of the time (and our personal differences), but they are essentially universal. They include the Mother, the Father, the Hero, the Heroine, the Lover, the Wanderer, the Wise Man, the Old Hag, the Saviour, the Victim and so on. The 22 Major Arcana invoke all of these archetypal images in one way or another.

Psychological dimension

Modern tarot reading has also developed from simple "fortune-telling" to being concerned with the psychological dimensions of divination. Ironically, those clichéd interpretations of the fortune-teller, like "a tall dark stranger is going to cross your path" are equally valid. After all, who is a tall dark stranger if not an archetypal personification of the "hero" in our Western world? "Tall dark stranger" ignites an inner reaction to the archetype that embodies love, mystery, danger and romance. And who is a "fortune-teller" if not someone who represents the energy of the archetypal witch, wizard, magician, clairvoyant in all of us?

What we project onto the tarot is exactly who we are. As Jung pointed out, by confronting the archetypal energies and freeing ourselves from their compulsive element, we can begin to take responsibility for individual choice and become who we truly are.

Meditation

With its rich archetypal imagery and symbolism, the tarot can easily be used for meditation. The tarot resonates to your intuition; it is up to you to open yourself to that intuition which is always there for you. Simply by concentrating on a card and letting the images flow freely through your mind, you will begin to develop your own powerful interpretation skills without having to resort to a book.

The meditative state exiles all those conscious thoughts, fears, worries and anxieties that can block the flow of archetypes and symbolism that speak to you. The dynamics of the unconscious flow deeply within us all, and accessing them is not always easy in our self-centered little worlds. But with meditation you can unlock the doors and access the deeper wisdom of the universe.

Remember, meditation isn't a non-experience; in fact, you will find that you become more in tune with your senses. Your hearing may be more acute, colors may seem more vivid, you smell the cards as well as touch them, and ultimately you touch and resonate with the hidden aspects of yourself.

Meditation is a great way to open yourself up to your unconscious.

Meditation step-by-step

There are no hard and fast rules to meditation, but relaxation is the key.

1 In a room where you won't be disturbed, find a comfortable sitting position. The most common is to sit cross-legged on the floor with your hands palm upward resting on your knees.

2 Draw a card from the deck or chose a specific card you like or want to know more about. Put the card face up in front of you or prop it against a wall where you can focus on it without straining your eyes.

3 Focus on the card. Become aware of your breathing.

Close your eyes and open your mind, body and soul to the tarot imagery.

4 As you inhale, try to let go of any thoughts that come to you except the awareness of your breathing. As you exhale begin to count; when you reach ten go back to one again to keep yourself focused. If you find that your mind begins to wander, begin at one again.

5 After a few minutes open your mind, body and soul to the tarot imagery. Focus on a color, one image, a number, or anything else specific on the card. As you breathe, gradually visualize that you are inside the card and are part of that world. Because you are entering the archetypal realms, you may meet "characters" that you know— friends, enemies, family, lovers who personify the quality of that particular card.

6 When you want, let go of the focus, connect with your breathing and close your eyes for a moment, then open them again. Move your gaze from the card and affirm to yourself that you are in harmony with the tarot and then return the card to the deck.

7 Let the images, ideas and feelings that you absorbed during the meditation stay with you. You will discover some insightful connections between the card and your current situation throughout the following few days.

Creating your own cards and spreads

After you have been using and reading the tarot for some time, and have become familiar with its symbols and archetypes, you may like to create your own set of cards. Likewise, once you have become familiar with a number of the standard layouts, you might find it a challenge to design your own layouts and establish your own sets of questions.

Designing your own deck

You might be inspired by just one theme or base your own deck on a metaphysical concept or belief. You don't have to be an artist to create your own unique deck of tarot cards. You don't even have to design all 78 cards either. You could just focus on the 22 Major Arcana, or simply create a set of 12 zodiac cards, one for each month of the year.

Perhaps you could use collage to make up your tarot images. Collect images that interest you and try to incorporate them into your designs. If you think you are a bit of an artist, try creating a rough sketch series of tarot images on a piece of paper first. Think about what the archetypes mean to you personally. What images stand out in your mind from the various decks you've seen around?

Creating your own spreads

After you have become fairly confident with using spreads, it is time to start developing your own layouts. There are many layouts in this book to choose from, but you can also adapt the ideas, layout and themes to create your own enriched versions. There are no rules, but you could perhaps base your ideas on a metaphysical pattern or structure—for example, the Tree of Life, the zodiac or the chakras.

Themes can be taken from the tarot cards themselves, maybe a "Hermit" spread or a "World" spread, and you can take your themes from numerical values, too. For example, a more complex spread might contain 22 cards. The number 22 is the number of unity. You could create a layout with 22 cards or two spreads side-by-side of 11 cards each. Each card would represent a factor in your life that needs to be expressed so that you will feel "whole" or feel unified in mind, body, soul and spirit.

Tarot mandalas

Alternatively, you can make your own tarot "mandala." This is simply a pattern formed from as many cards as you like, which can either become a reading itself or simply a beautiful geometrical image of cards which you can then use for meditational purposes. You can add cards or take away cards as you wish. You can transform the pattern, change the images and subsequently work your own ideas and feelings out through the changing pattern. Below is an example of how to create a tarot mandala.

Shuffle the cards as usual, and then without choosing specific cards just take one card at a time from the top of the pack and lay them out from a central core in any geometrical pattern that you feel works for you. It could be based on circles, crosses, numbers, triangles, squares, spirals, or crop-circle patterns; but the important thing is to keep laying out the cards until you feel the mandala resonates to something inner within you. This mandala symbolizes the patterns of energy that flow through your unconscious. Each card is an expression of your current feelings, moods or desires.

Adapting three-card spreads

If you have a specific question or issue, then you can adapt the three-card spreads used in this book for simple question-and-answer problems. A three-card spread can represent many situations—for example: past, present and future; love, career, money; secrets, wishes, needs; tomorrow, the day after, next week.

The main thing to remember is not to make your spreads too complex to begin with or you will find it difficult to interpret them. Finally, always write down or make a note of your designs, and remember if some don't work then don't continue to use them; the best tarot spreads are the ones that work best for you.

You might want to start by inventing a geometrical pattern with the cards and decide what each layout concerns. You could have anger spreads, love spreads, energy spreads, transformation spreads, goals and passion spreads. In fact, use your own issues to guide you because the tarot mirror is all about you. If you want to examine a situation in detail, then a layout that includes past, present and future positions is usually very revealing. You can see what influences or experiences in the past have led up to current circumstances and decide how to deal with them.

Pair and group work

The tarot is a wonderful tool for self-development, but it doesn't always have to be a solitary experience. In fact, sometimes it is less subjective and more revealing if you do some tarot work in the company of others.

If you have already tried the relationship layouts with a partner or friend, you will know that working with someone directly can push your psychological buttons. But it is ultimately rewarding.

Another way to use the tarot between two friends is to take turns reading as if for a client. This is good practice if you do ever want to read other people's tarot, because it makes you realize what it's like to be the client. You draw three cards and lay them face up on the table; as each card is chosen, your friend interprets your cards in relation to you. You must not say a word. Afterward, discuss what reactions you had to your friend's interpretation of your card in relation to you. Did it feel uncomfortable, were you secretly pleased about what she said, would you rather have spoken up and said what you believed it meant because you think your interpretation is the real one? Then switch roles and repeat the challenge.

Group work

It can be extremely stimulating to explore the relationship between the people in a group. Obviously, too many cooks spoil the broth, so the ideal number for this kind of work is between three and seven.

Make sure everyone has a turn at shuffling the cards. Usually someone will play the role of team leader and therefore be responsible for laying the cards out in an overlapping line or holding them in a fan shape in order for the cards to be chosen.

Next, each person chooses a card and places it face down on the table or floor. When everyone has finished choosing random cards, the first person turns over his or her card, which will relate to the person sitting to their left, and so on. Each person gives their interpretation out loud, saying what this card reveals to them about their neighbor. This is highly interactive and, although very challenging, can also be great fun. It can really help you discover more about yourself and the people you know.

Using the tarot with other people can be great fun and very rewarding.

Glossary

Arcana/Arcanum
The Major Arcana and the Minor Arcana are the two distinctly different series of cards in a Tarot deck. *Arcanum* is a Latin word meaning "secret." Its plural form is Arcana, so Major and Minor Arcana mean "big secrets" and "little secrets."

Archetypes
Those instinctual universal forces or patterns of behaviour that operate autonomously in the depths of the human psyche.

Aries
The first sign of the zodiac. Ruled by the planet Mars, Aries is associated with potency, will, daring and impulse.

Art of memory
A device invented by the ancient Greeks to impress images on the mind to help with symbolic association. The later Renaissance memory systems were subsequently linked to magical talismans and occult practices.

Astrological year
Beginning at 0 degrees Aries, the astrological year aligns to the path of the sun (the ecliptic) as it appears to move through each section of the zodiac. The last degree of Pisces marks the end of the astrological year, thus completing its 360 degree cycle.

Astrology
An ancient system of divination that studies the patterns and placement of the planets of the solar system as they appear to travel through the zodiac belt.

Blockage card
A "blockage card" is a tarot card that crosses or sits at right angles on top of another card.

Book of Thoth

According to the 18th century scholar, Gebelin, the Tarot is in fact an ancient Egpytian book, the Book of Thoth, saved from the ruins of burning temples. Thoth was both a god, equivalent to the Greek Hermes, and an early Egpytian king, believed to be the inventor of hieroglyphics and mystical letters or symbols which occult scholars recognized in the Tarot.

Celtic Cross

One of the most popular and oldest spreads for Tarot reading. A.E. Waite identified this method in 1910, but little is known of its origins. The spread is in a form of a mystical stone cross found throughout Ireland. The cards are laid out in a cross with a vertical column representing the human spiritual quest.

Chakra

Many Eastern traditions maintain that a system of energy flows through the body linked by seven or more energy centres known as chakras.

Divination

Divination literally means "to foresee, foretell or predict," and comes from the Latin word *divinus* meaning "to be inspired by the gods." Many cultures throughout the world have "foretold" the future using anything from tossed twigs, coins and tea leaves to patterns in puddles after the rain. The desire to know what "will be" is a very strong human drive.

Elements

The four "elements" are used in astrology and in Jungian psychology. In astrology they are divided up into the Fire signs Aries, Leo and Sagittarius; the Air signs Gemini, Libra, and Aquarius; the Water signs Cancer, Scorpio and Pisces; and the Earth signs Taurus, Virgo and Capricorn. Jung linked them to the basic ways of experiencing the world—Fire for intuition, Air for thinking, Water for feeling and Earth for sensation. The elements represent qualities and characteristics in people.

Freemason

A member of an international order of fellowship, criticized for their secrecy and supposed occult rituals and practices. The original "free masons" were 14th century skilled stone masons who used secret signs to communicate.

Future outcome card

A card that is placed in a position and signifies the outcome of the issue at stake. A future outcome card defines the next step or stage of your journey.

Kabballah

The Kabbalah is an ancient esoteric and magical pathway from the Hebrew tradition which offers profound wisdom and spiritual insight. The word *Kabbalah* is derived from a Hebrew word meaning "to receive." The core element to the Kabbalah is the Tree of Life, a blueprint for the universe which attempts to reveal the interconnected aspects of all life.

Knights Templar

Founded as the Poor Knights of Christ and the Temple of Solomon in 1118, a religious and military protection league for pilgrims to the Holy Land. The order became powerful and wealthy, and was suppressed in 1312 but continued to operate in secrecy.

Magi

Plural of *Magus*, a Latin word from old Persian "magush," meaning magician.

Numerology

The art of divination using numbers that were considered pivotal to everything that goes on in the universe. The primary numbers, 1–9 each vibrate to a different frequency, and these vibrations echo throughout the universe. This "music of the spheres" was an expression of the heavenly bodies, which had their own numerical value and harmonic vibration.

Occult

From a latin word *occultus* meaning hidden, mysterious. Used from the 15th century as a verb to mean to conceal. Favoured in the 19th century to describe supernatural and magical beliefs and practices.

Order of the Golden Dawn

One of the most influential occultist groups founded in 1888 by William Wynn Westcott, a doctor and master mason, along with a flamboyant character in Victorian society called Samuel Mathers. Drawing on many different esoteric beliefs, Mathers fused Egyptian magical systems with both medieval magic texts and eastern esoteric beliefs to create a workable magic system which also incorporated the Kabballah.

Papi

Plural form of the Latin word *papa*, meaning pope, father, bishop. The first 35 cards of the Minchiate deck were called "papi," and numbered with roman numerals. Possibly to infer an affinity to Christian links rather than anything mystical. However, it could also be a corruption of a latin interjection spelt "papae" meaning "wonderful!" or "how strange!"

Pentacles

Magical object or talisman usually disc-shaped and used as a symbol for the Element Earth. One of the four suits in Tarot, often referred to also as coins or discs. The word derives from the medieval Latin word, "pentaculum," related to the pentagram or five pointed mystical and magical star.

Pips

A small shape or symbol on suits in Tarot packs and normal playing cards to define the nature of the suit. For example, the Five of Swords will show five swords and the number five, whereas most modern day tarot packs have a different pictorial image for each numbered card.

Projection

Projection is an unconscious process whereby we see in the person, thing, object, experience or event those potentials, flaws, hates and loves that actually belong to us. We create a world around us of the characters, myths, heroes and villains who are part of the very theatre hidden within our own depths.

Psyche

In Greek mythology, Psyche was the personification of the soul. Also used nowadays to describe the human soul in psychological fields, and derived from a Greek word meaning, "air, breath, life, spirit."

Quintessential Number

Derived from a Latin word meaning "fifth essence," quintessential has been used to imply the most perfect example, or the finest quality. The quintessential number is a perfect number symbolically, formed by adding all the other numbers of a numerological reading together. This "Quintessential Number" becomes the overall guide and purpose of the reading in question.

Synchronicity

The belief that everything in the universe is interconnected, and that events, patterns in the zodiac, the tea cup, in another person's life or anywhere on Earth are all an interface of an invisible force. In other words, the randomness of divination is itself part of this process.

The psychologist Carl Jung coined the word *synchronicity* to describe such meaningful coincidences. He believed the tarot card we select is prompted by something inner that needs to be expressed or must become manifest in the outer world at that moment.

Symbol

A sign of recognition or a token, rooted in an ancient Greek word meaning "something thrown together."

Tarot

Some sources suggest the word *tarot* is a derivative of the name of the god Thoth, who was the Egyptian god of magic and words. Others believe it has Hebrew or Arabic origins, possibly a corruption of the "torah," the book of law. And again some commentators believe it could partly be an anagram of *rota*, a Latin word meaning "wheel."

You now card

The first card laid down is usually called the "you now" card and signifies the current state of the questioner and surrounding issues.

Zoroastrianism

Founded by Zoroaster in the 6th century BC, a monotheistic religion of ancient Persia, which became a cult among late 19th century occultists as a dualistic cosmology of truth versus untruth.

Index

Index

what will happen on this day? 354

Acknowledgments

Tarot images ©Lo Scarabeo.

Other images: AKG, London 34. **Corbis UK Limited** 22, 61, 79, 303; /Bettmann 21, 25; /E. O. Hoppe 20; /Michael Nicholson 17; /The Cover Story 56–57.
Creatas13. **Getty Images**/Altrendo Images 383. **ImageSource** 78, 302, 375.
Octopus Publishing Group Limited 18, 60, 256–257, 278, 331, 370 top center; /Walter Gardiner 76; /Mike Hemsley at Walter Gardiner Photographers 330, 376; /Andy Komorowski 370 top left, 370 top right; /Ian Parsons 7, 8, 24, 46, 49, 53, 65; /Mike Prior 47, 368 top; /William Reavell 15; /Guy Ryecart 27; /Russell Sadur 58 left, 368 bottom; /Gareth Sambidge 23; /Ian Wallace 52; /Mark Winwood 29, 258.
Photolibrary Group 54–55. **The Picture Desk Limited/Art Archive**/Eileen Tweedy 38. **TopFoto** 37.

Executive Editor Sandra Rigby
Managing Editor Clare Churly
Executive Art Editor Sally Bond
Designer Julie Francis
Picture Librarian Sophie Delpech
Production Manager Louise Hall